George Cuthbert Blaxland

Mayflower Essays

On the Story of the Pilgrim Fathers

George Cuthbert Blaxland

Mayflower Essays
On the Story of the Pilgrim Fathers

ISBN/EAN: 9783337079246

Printed in Europe, USA, Canada, Australia, Japan

Cover: Foto ©Thomas Meinert / pixelio.de

More available books at **www.hansebooks.com**

"MAYFLOWER" ESSAYS

ON

The Story of the Pilgrim Fathers

AS TOLD IN GOVERNOR BRADFORD'S MS.

HISTORY OF THE PLIMOTH PLANTATION

WITH A REPRODUCTION OF CAPTAIN JOHN SMITH'S

MAP OF NEW ENGLAND

BY

G.^{ev} CUTHBERT BLAXLAND M.A.

SOMETIME SCHOLAR OF PEMBROKE COLLEGE OXFORD
AND DOMESTIC CHAPLAIN TO THE LATE BISHOP OF LONDON

LONDON
WARD & DOWNEY LIMITED
12 YORK BUILDINGS ADELPHI W.C.
1896

PRINTED BY
SPOTTISWOODE AND CO., NEW-STREET SQUARE
LONDON

PREFACE

T HESE Essays are the offspring of an interest
which the present writer learned to feel in
the Bradford MS. at a time when he had
the privilege of being its custodian. That
interest, dormant for many years, has been
revived by the recent publication in fac-simile
of the priceless document, whereby that
which was formerly the privilege of the few
has become the general property of the
reading world. It has now been made possible
for anyone who desires to do so not only to
read the story as it was written, but even to
see with his own eyes, as it were, the very
strokes of Governor Bradford's pen, and
almost to stand by him as he traces, with
conscientious pains, his old, yet living, story.

Such an occasion may, it is hoped, justify the issue of these "scribbled writings," which, while they lay claim to no originality or research outside the manuscript itself, may yet impart to his readers some of the interest and profitable enjoyment which the author has himself derived from its time-honoured pages.

CONTENTS

CONTENTS

"MAYFLOWER" ESSAYS

I

EXILES FOR CONSCIENCE SAKE

GOVERNOR BRADFORD'S story of PLIMOTH PLANTATION may truly be regarded, in conception and design, as a prose Epic. To say this does not imply that there is in it any conscious selection or arrangement of the materials to produce an artistic effect, or that there is any attempt to work up the subject to an artificial climax. On the contrary, nothing could be more simple and unstudied than the general course of the narrative. Bradford's story unfolds itself according to the modest and unambitious rule which he sets before himself at the beginning.

B

*And first of y*ᵉ* occasion, and Inducements,
therunto; the which that I may truly unfould,
I must begine at y*ᶠ* very roote & rise of y*ᶠ* same.
The which I shall endevor to manefest in a
plaine stile; with singuler regard unto y*ᵉ*
simple trueth in all things, at least as near as
my slender judgmente can attaine the same.*

He leads his readers through a mass of
details, of correspondence on commercial
matters, of long-winded legal documents, all
of great historical interest, yet many of
them decidedly prosaic in character. He
omits nothing which truth requires to be
told. He adopts after the first Introductory
Book, the most inartistic of all styles, the
style of the simple annalist, recording the
events of each year by themselves, as
though they were written in a journal. Yet
still there is evidence to show that the
materials were not really put together, in
their present form, until a later period.
Bradford wrote at a time when the result
to which events were tending had been

attained, and was actually realised before his eyes. And the consciousness of that attained result, great and honourable as it was, filling his mind, tinges his retrospect of the preceding events at many points. It becomes a pervading spirit, giving life and purpose to the whole body. And so without art or effort, yet not without intention, his record of events from year to year, as God in His Providence had ordered them, clothed in a language which, though often homely, is never petty or undignified, but rather full of unstudied grace, and infused with the poetry of deep feeling and unaffected religion, becomes a true Epic. It is an Epic of the Ways of God with Man. The little one has become a thousand. The cause once despised and persecuted has attained to honour and triumph. Step by step through crushing disasters, through difficulty and opposition, through misrepresentation and persecution, patient perseverance and heroic faithfulness to truth have vindicated their cause. The exiles for conscience sake, seeking only to follow the path set before them, without knowing whither it would tend, have come to be the honour and example of a new world.

Such is Bradford's conception of his subject. It is a history which does not stand alone in the annals of the human race. In every age there have been men who have endured persecution, and faced difficulty for the truth, as they have conceived it, men by whose single-minded and self-sacrificing devotion to their cause, the world has been enriched and ennobled, and of whom it has not been worthy. But even were such instances many times more numerous than they are, the cost of heroism to the sufferer would still be the same, and equally deserving of our gratitude and honour. Nor is it needful that we should be in full accord with Bradford's theological principles, that we should adopt his estimate of the exclusive righteousness of his cause, or of the character of his enemies, in alliance, as it seemed to him, with the powers of darkness, in order to sympathise with his enthusiasm, or to give to him, and the "*pore, persecuted Church*" whose sufferings he shared, our ungrudging tribute of admiration and praise. Persecution is an ugly and shameful thing, by whomsoever it is practised, and makes a blot upon the fair fame of those who have been guilty of it, which is not easily wiped off by their successors.   But history compels us to acknowledge that, at a time when all persecuted, the blame rests upon all, and not upon any section or party.   And similarly all Englishmen must feel a pride in, and cherish as a precious possession, the memory of men who were true to their consciences, let the cost be what it might, and who pursued their aim undaunted, though the difficulties were well-nigh overwhelming. The lasting and permanent value, for Englishmen generally, of the struggle in which the *Pilgrim Fathers*, to use the name by which posterity has honoured their memory, played the men, lies not in the particular form of Church discipline or doctrine for which they contended, but in their assertion of the great principle that conscience is free, that it is not to be coerced, that neither Church, nor state, nor individuals may use compulsion, much less vindictive terrorism, to tear away men's hearts from convictions for which they are answerable to God only. For this principle, which they instinctively felt, perhaps, rather than saw, to be true in their own case, the Pilgrim Fathers made their stand, in the strength of passive and unretaliating endurance while at home, and in the resolution to be free at any cost, when they embraced exile. For this mankind is their debtor. Whether they recognised the whole scope of the issue, and its application to others also, is another question into which we do not now enter. Our object is to reflect, if it may be, something of the picture which Bradford so graphically and ingenuously draws. Assuredly the Pilgrim Fathers owe much to their historian.

The Bradford MS. is practically the main source from which our knowledge of the

planting of *Plymouth Plantation*, and the events
which led to it, is derived. Other writers who,
in the next generations, became the historians
of the Colony, do little more than borrow
from Bradford, adopting his words and
phrases, with the addition, often by no means
an improvement, of occasional amplifications
and insertions. It is well known that the
discovery and identification of the MS.,
after its long and unaccountable burial in the
Library of Fulham Palace, were due to the
correspondence of extracts quoted from it by
Bishop Wilberforce with passages, known
to have been transcribed from its pages by
Bradford's successors. What adds an especial
interest, is that it is the history of a most
eventful time, written by the man who had
the principal share in making that history.
For it was Bradford's influence, more than
anything else, that governed the Colony after
its first plantation. And there is, further,
for us the additional charm that in its simple,
unlaboured narrative, its homely phrases and
vivid details, we have presented to us a living

picture of the thoughts, ways, words pre-
valent at the time. We have also a portrait
of a man who, while reflecting much of the
contemporary Puritan character at its best,
serious, Godfearing, resolute, added thereto
a warmth of affection, a depth of feeling, a
wealth of human sympathies, a vigour of
judgment and action, enlivened by twinkles
of humour, which were all his own.

In order to understand the position of the
early Independents, we must briefly glance
at the course which the Reformation
had hitherto taken in England. On the
Continent the burning question of religion,
which form should predominate, whether
Catholic or Protestant, had arisen, been
fought out, and settled, all within or very
nearly within the course of the sixteenth
century. Thus Germany had been divided
into Catholic and Protestant by the Treaty of
Passau in 1552. And although there was yet
one more conflict to come—for while Bradford was building up his colony in New
England, Germany was passing through

the throes of the Thirty Years' War—yet the *status quo* remained practically unchanged. In France the Huguenots had struggled for equality, and in spite of the Massacre of St. Bartholomew's had even seen a King of their own ascend the throne. But that King had been obliged to buy Paris with a mass, and the Huguenots had to be content with the right to exist, given by the Edict of Nantes in 1598, as a settlement of the question. The Low Countries had contended stubbornly for their independence, political and spiritual, against Granvelle and Alva and all the power of Spain ; and although what is now Belgium was permanently lost to them, and, at the time when the exiles from Scrooby arrived, Holland was resting from its struggle on the precarious security of a twelve years' truce (commencing in 1609), yet there Protestantism had really and permanently won the day.

In England alone there had as yet been no war, though blood had been shed on the scaffold and at the stake, and the religious question had not been settled. The Roman

supremacy had indeed been finally abolished.
But what form the National Christianity
would take, remained still at issue. The
clouds were gathering, soon about to break
upon the country in the storm of the Civil
War, of which the Pilgrims would hear the
distant rumours in their home beyond the
sea. But, meanwhile, the conflict was being
carried on within the fold of the National
Church. The refugees from the Marian
persecutions, who had returned eager to
impress upon the Church the principles
which they had learned in Holland,
Germany, and Switzerland, had made no
open breach with it. The influence of
Elizabeth, and the threat of foreign invasion,
tended to hold the divergent elements
together. The disappointment felt by the
more advanced Reformers, when James I.
and the Hampton Court conference maintained the Edwardian settlement, had tended
to accentuate differences. But the Puritans
still maintained their union with the Church,
which they desired to convert to their views

from within, and not to overthrow. Both
Puritan and high-churchman alike looked
with equal disfavour upon those who inclined
to separation. Some attempts had been
made to form independent bodies. The
first advocacy of these principles is usually
associated with the name of Robert Browne,
who separated from the Church about 1580,
though it appears that there existed independent congregations still earlier. But
Nonconformity had as yet made comparatively but little progress. The name of
"*Brownist*" was a term of reproach which
even the Plymouth Colonists, some years
after their emigration, showed a disposition
to evade, though they did not actually deny
it.[1]   And the Nonconformists generally seem

---

[1] In the year 1625 the Adventurers allege as one of the
reasons for breaking up the Company, that the Colonists
have dissembled with them about the French discipline, &c.,
and that though they deny the name of Brownists yet they
practise the same, and therefore they (the Adventurers)
would sin against God in building up such a people. It is
noticeable that the Colonists in their reply maintain their
liberty to differ from the French discipline. But the charge of
the "*scandallous name of Brownist*" they leave unanswered.
—Bradford MS., p. 134.

to have been in the position of men who
have no friends, exposed to coldness, opposition, and even persecution from every side.

Such was the situation of affairs at the
time when Bradford takes up the story of the
pore persecuted Church, to which he was so
ardently attached. He is indignant at the
"*warrs and oppositions Satan hath raised,
maintained and continued against the saincts.*"
And especially is he indignant with those *seem-
ing reformed* professors, who had stirred up
discord among the refugees on the Continent,
and then had brought the same contention to
England under "*gracious Queene Elizabeth.*"
It is they, he declares, who by their com-
promise with Episcopacy have betrayed their
cause ; they have incensed the Queen against
the faithful few ; they, "*to cast contempte the
more upon ye sincere servants of God,*" have
"*opprobriously and most injuriously*" given
unto, and "*imposed upon them that name of
Puritans, which [it] is said the Nouatians (out
of prid) did assume and take unto themselves.*"
And so it is they who are responsible for the per-

secutions which have befallen God's servants.
The whole passage is characteristic of the
impetuous vigour with which Bradford could
write when thoroughly roused. And not less
vehement is the description of the wrongs
and injuries done to the two congregations
formed out of sundry towns and villages,
"*some in Notingamshire, some of Lincollin-
shire, and some of Yorkshire, where they
border nearest togeather*," with one of which
that of Scrooby[1] is identified. It is not necessary to dwell more in detail upon this, the
least pleasing part of our subject. Nor is it
proposed to follow the steps of those migrations, first to Leyden, and then across the
Atlantic to New England, by which the
Pilgrims became the pioneers of a great
religious and colonial enterprise in the New
World. Their story has been fully told by
others. Our purpose is rather to try and
gather out of Bradford's chronicle an esti-

---

[1] The name of Scrooby is not mentioned. But this allusion to the junction of the three counties, coupled with the
mention in Mr. Brewster's life (p. 255) of the place of meeting
as "*a manor of y͡e Bishop's*," has led to the identification.

mate of some of the causes which led to the honourable success which they did ultimately achieve. From the Proem of the Epic we transfer our point of view to the culmination, and cast a backward glance upon some features of its progress.

We cannot but be profoundly impressed by the greatness of the difficulties through which, at the outset, the Pilgrims had to force their way. Their forlorn estate in England, the difficulties of their first embarkation, the hardships they encountered in Holland, the discouragements which attended their first appeals for means to plant a Colony, and the hard terms on which they had to purchase that assistance. These were the commencement. Then the necessity to abandon one of the ships and part of the company at Plymouth, the visitation of sickness which broke out shortly after their landing, and reduced their numbers by nearly half, followed by the neglect and speedy abandonment of the undertaking by the Adventurers, leaving them in weak-ness and isolation to cope with the rigorous

climate and unknown possibilities of their
new home—these complete the catalogue of
adversities, of disaster upon disaster, under
which we can but marvel that they did not
succumb. For it was by no means a fore-
gone conclusion that a Colony at that period
should succeed. On the contrary, success was
the exception ; the whole coast of the continent was strewn with the wrecks of previous
failures. An interesting comparison, by way
of contrast, is afforded by the history of the
shortlived Colony planted two years later in
Massachusetts Bay. It was planted in a
spot which had natural advantages superior
to those of Plymouth, at a more favourable
time of year, and, what makes the comparison
more instructive, it was sent out by the same
Mr. Weston who had taken the leading part
among the Adventurers in forwarding the
colonists to Plymouth. Thus they had the
advantage of the experience that had been
acquired ; they were able, further, to avail
themselves of Plymouth as a *pied-à-terre*
while fixing their abode. The first party of

colonists are described as "*sixty lusty men*,"
probably by no means inferior in physical
strength and hardiness to those of Plymouth.
And they came out in arrogant confidence of
success.   And yet the first winter brought
them to ruin.   Just one picture, in the words
of Bradford, may be given, and will serve to
show the possibilities of disaster to which
these early Colonies were exposed.

*It may be thought strang that these people
should fall to these extremities in so short a
time, being left competently provided when
y*ᵉ* ship left them, and had an addition by that
moyetie of corn that was got by trade, besids
much they gott of y*ᵉ* Indeans wher they lived
by one means & other.   It must needs be their
great disorder, for they spent excesseivly whilst
they had, or could get it, and, it may be, wasted
parte away amongst y*ᵉ* Indeans (for he y*ᵗ* was
their cheef was taxed by some amongst them,
for keeping Indean women, how truly I know
not).   And after they begane to come into
wants, many sould away their cloathes, and*

bed coverings; others (so base were they) be-came servants to ye Indeans, and would cutt them woode, and fetch them water, for a cap full of corne; others fell to plaine stealing, both night & day from ye Indeans, of which they greevosly complained. In ye end they came to that misery, that some starved & dyed with could & hunger; one in geathering shell fish was so weake as he stuck fast in ye mudd, and was found dead in ye place. At last most of them left their dwellings, & scatered up & downe in ye woods, & by ye water sids, wher they could find ground nuts & clames, hear 6 and ther ten. By which their cariages they became contemned & scorned of ye Indeans; and they begane greatly to insulte over them, in a most in-solente maner. Insomuch y^t many times as they lay thus scatered abrod, and had set on a pot with ground nuts, or shell-fish, when it was ready the Indeans would come and eate it up; and when night came, wheras some of them had a sorie blanket, or such like, to lappe them selves in, the Indeans would take it, and let

C

y *other lye all night in the could; so as their*
condition was very lamentable. Yea in y *end*
they were faine to hange one of their men,
whom they could not reclaime from stealing,
to give y *Indeans contente.*

The result was that a conspiracy was
formed amongst the Indians, which might
have resulted in the extermination of the
English, if the Plymouth people had not
received information, and interfered to the
rescue of their unworthy fellow-countrymen.
The same disgraceful and disastrous history
was enacted in the same place when Captain
John Wolastone, (*a man of pretie parts* himself), made a second attempt, about 1624, to
establish a Colony in Massachusetts Bay. A
share in the management was left in the unworthy hands of one Morton, a man of
more craft than honestie (who had been a
kind of petiefogger of Furnefels Inne), with
the result that by dissoluteness of conduct, and reckless treatment of the Indians,
they were reduced to great personal peril,
and became a standing danger to the sur-

rounding colonists, so that Plymouth was again obliged to interfere. From the many other instances of the lawless violence, the selfishness, the unprincipled recklessness which seem to have been only too common, if not the rule, among the sailors, fishermen and adventurers by whom colonial enterprise at that period was carried on, we turn with relief to the picture of the quiet, self-restrained, law-abiding God-fearing demeanour of the colonists at Plymouth. It was in these qualities that their strength and the secret of their success lay, though their material power and wealth were small.

The principles by which they were influenced on starting, and on which they based their hopes of success, are well set forth by themselves in the "Articles of Inducement" drawn up when they were seeking to leave Holland: and if the establishment of a Colony on these principles was not altogether a new experiment, yet the carrying of them out was an object lesson to the world.

1. *We veryly beleeve & trust y* Lord is
with us, unto whom & whose service we have
given our selves in many trialls; and that He
will graciously prosper our Indeavour, according to the simplicitie of our harts therin.*

2*ly We are well weaned from y* dellicate
milke of our mother countrie, and enured to y*
difficulties of a strange and hard land; which
yet in great parte we have by patience overcome.*

3*ly The people are, for the body of them,
industrious, and frugall (we thinke we may
safly say) as any company of people in the
world.*

4*ly We are knite togeather, as a body, in
a most stricte, & sacred bond and covenante of
the Lord; of the violation wherof we make
great conscience, and by vertue wherof, we doe
hould our selves straitly tied to all care of
each others good, and of y* whole by every one,
and so mutually.*

*Lastly, it is not with us, as with other
men, whom small things can discourage, or
small discontentments cause to wish themselves
at home againe; we knowe our entertainmente*

*in England, and in Holand we shall much
prejudice both our arts, & means by removall;
where (if we should be driven to returne) we
should not hope to recover our present helps,
and comforts. Neither indeed looke ever (for
our selves) to attaine unto y* like in any other
place, during our lives, which are now draw-
ing towards their periods.*

It must indeed be recognised that a
great part of their success was due to the
wisdom with which they were governed.
But the credit of good government, in a
voluntary community such as theirs, must be
given to the good sense of the governed,
who accepted and upheld it, as well as to
the governors who by the will of the community administered it. They had been
trained in habits of self-government by their
Church organisation, and it is very striking to
observe how from the time when, in the
ships at Southampton, they elected their
governors and assistants, and onwards
through their history, the instincts of law

and order never failed them, preserving them
from confusion and panic even in positions
of great anxiety. The voice which everyone
had in the management of public matters
was a fact, and not merely a theory. And
the governor, who respected that right, had
the strength of an intelligent consensus of
judgment and support behind him. Even
in the complicated questions involved in the
transfer of the property of the company, first
to all the colonists as shareholders, and then to
the seven "undertakers" who hired it of them
for six years, Bradford tells us that all the
members were consulted, had the proposed
steps explained to them, and gave their
consent. The complicated arrangement
which ensued when the lands were divided
by lot, which provided, for the sake of
equality, that "*whose lotts so ever should fall
next ye towne or most conveniente for nearnes,
should take to them a neighboure or tow,
whom they best liked, & should suffer them
to plant corne wth them for 4 years, and
afterwards they might use as much of theirs*

for as long time, if they would," [1] could only
have been conceived as likely to be a
workable theory in a community where
common participation in the management
had trained the people to confidence in their
laws, and in one another.

It is true that even with their unusually
developed sense of public spirit, and of the
necessity for subordinating individual advantage to the general good, a system of
absolute Communism proved a failure. Such
a system does not seem to have been a
success even among the Christians of the
Apostolic Age. It was not of their own
will that the Plymouth colonists first adopted
it ; it was forced upon them by the Adventurers. A loyal attempt to adhere to the
system, by which the community was the
holder of all property, was made for about a
year and a half. But stress of scarcity
forced them into adopting a more productive
system, so far at any rate as to allow that
" *they should set corne every man for his*

---

[1] Bradford MS., p. 146.

owne particuler, and in that regard trust to themselves." And the result in making "*all hands very industrious*" and in promoting friendliness and plenty, was, on Bradford's authority, a marked success. The fact that, under circumstances so unusually favourable, the Communistic system nevertheless broke down, is full of significance for students of social questions, and Bradford's description and his comments thereon are well worthy to be quoted in full, as a characteristic specimen both of his judgment and of his style.

The experience that was had in this comone course and condition, tried sundrie years, and that amongst godly, and sober men, may well evince, the vanitie of that conceite of Plato's, & other ancients, applauded by some of later times, that ye taking away of propertie, and bring^{ing} in comunitie, into a comone wealth, would make them happy, and florishing, as if they were wiser then God. For this comunitie, (so farr as it was) was found to breed much con-

fusion, & discontent, and retard much Im-bloyment, that would have been to their benefite and comforte. For ye yong-men that were most able and fitte for labour and service, did repine that they should spend their time, & strength to worke for other men's wives, and children, without any recompence. The strong, or man of parts, had no more in de-. vision of victails, & cloaths, then he that was weake, and not able to doe a quarter ye other could, this was thought Injuestice. The aged and graver men to be ranked, and equalised, in labours, and victails, cloaths, &c., with ye meaner, & yonger sorte, thought it some Indignite, and disrespect unto them. And for men's wives to be commanded to doe servise for other men, as dressing ther meate, washing their cloaths, &c., they deem it a kind of slaverie, neither could many husbands well brooke it. Upon ye poynte all being to have alike, and all to doe alike, they thought them selves in ye like condition, and one as good as another ; and so if it did not cut of. those relations, that God hath set amongest *men ; yet it did at least much diminish, and take of, y*e* mutuall respects, that should be preserved amongst them. And would have bene worse if they had been men of another condition. Let none objecte this is men's coruption, and nothing to y*e* course itselfe ; I answer seeing all men have this coruption in them, God in his wisdome saw another course fiter for them.*

The failure of Communism notwithstanding, it was the spirit of sympathy and mutual assistance, manifested at the first when they had to nurse one another in sickness (contrasted with the unfeeling selfishness of the sailors, who formed the crew of the *Mayflower*, in like condition), and which held them together through weal and woe, even when plotters like Lyford and Oldham tried to foment divisions among them, that formed the first element of their strength.

A second point to be noted is the high standard of morality which was throughout maintained. We hear on one occasion when

---

[1] Bradford MS., pp. 96-97.

the stress of famine was very sore, and the Colony was reduced to an allowance of a quarter of a pound of bread per day, that thefts of corn took place, and the thieves when discovered had to be *well whipt*. But this was exceptional. The unruly conduct of parties of men who from time to time visited the Colony was a source of great annoyance. The Puritan theory of the identity of Church and State, requiring that the law should regulate the private morals of individuals, led on several occasions to persons (visitors) suspected of immoral relations being packed out of the Colony with all despatch. One grievous outbreak of vice caused anxious communications between the Colonies of Salem and Plymouth, and offenders were visited with all the severity of the Levitical law. But it is significant that the first execution for murder did not occur till 1630. It caused, we read, great sadness among the people, and was not carried out without anxious consultation with Mr. Winthrop of Boston, and others who agreed that

the murderer should be executed, and the
land purged from blood.   The first house for
a prison was built in 1638.   We meet with
curious instances of the strictness of Puritan
discipline, as for instance in the stopping of
games in the street on Christmas Day 1621,
and in the incidental mention that "*every
Lord's day some are apointed to visite suspected places, & if any be found idling, and
neglecte ye hearing of ye word (through
idlenes or profanes), they are punished for y^e
same.*"   And Bradford in another place passes
severe strictures, as upon gross excesses
of dissoluteness and profanity, so also upon
the "*idle or Idoll Maypolle.*"   But even if
occasionally somewhat overstrained, and
wanting in proportion, this high regard for
purity and righteousness characterising them,
in common with the other early Puritans,
constituted one of the chief bonds of union
and strength among the Plymouth Pilgrims.

And this high regard for Christian uprightness and charity was manifested in
their dealings with the natives also, a circum-

stance which while it tended much to their
safety and success, is also a noble feature in
their colonial history, when compared with
the conduct of some English settlers in other
places and in later times. The corn which the
second exploring party from the ship found
at Pamet creek, and took for their pressing
need, was scrupulously paid for, when the
owners were found, six months later. When
Corbitant by his threatened violence to their
friends, Hobamack and Squanto, provoked
strong measures, an expedition of armed
men was sent with orders "*if they found
that Squanto was killed to cut of Corbitant's head; but not to hurt any but those
that had a hand in it.*" And when some of
the Indians were wounded through misun-
derstanding, the colonists brought them to
Plymouth, had their wounds dressed and
cured, and then sent them home. Their
kindness to Hobomack in his sickness was
requited by the revelation of the conspiracy
which might have broken out upon them to
their destruction. Kindness and justice was,

indeed, the best policy in their time of weakness, but unscrupulous men do not generally perceive or act upon the principle. And it is a striking and honourable instance of the righteous justice of their dealings with the Indians, that in the year 1638, when they had no such great danger to fear, three Englishmen were executed for the murder of one Indian, in spite of the dissatisfaction caused among many of the community, "*who murmured that any English should be put to death for Indians.*"[1] Another noble instance of Christian conduct deserves honourable mention. An offshoot of the Plymouth Colony was established at Connecticut, and in the year 1634 the Indians round about their settlement were visited with a fearful infliction of small-pox, which cut them off almost to a man, "*so that they were not able to help one another, no not to make a fire, nor to fetch a little water to drinke, nor any to burie the dead. . . . But those of ye English house (though at first they were afraid*

[1] Bradford MS., p. 228.

of ye infection) yet seeing their woefull and sadd condition, and hearing their pitiful cries and lamentations, they had compassion of them and daly fetched them wood and water, and made them fires, gott them victualls whilst they lived, and buried them when they dyed." Not without reason does our true-hearted, God-fearing author add his witness to the "*marvellous godness and providens of God*," in that "*not one of ye English was so much as sicke or in ye least measure tainted with this disease, though they daly did these offices for them, for many weeks togeather.*" [1]

And so we pause in our review of the causes by which the Pilgrim Fathers of New Plymouth were able to bring their Colony through storm and trouble to a position of stability and success, where so many failed. The causes lay in the men themselves, in their resolution, their industry, their sober self-control, their faithfulness to one another, and their maintenance of a high standard of

[1] Bradford MS., p. 204

righteousness in their dealings with their fellow-colonists and with the Indians. They succeeded because they deserved to succeed. They had had in the letter of Mr. Robinson,[1] addressed to them from Leyden at their departure, wise and noble counsel, and of this teaching they had been worthy disciples. The qualities for which we admire them and by which they deserved and won success sprang from a root which lay yet deeper. It sprang from a sincere devotion to the service of God and the belief in His sustaining power and protecting arm. The spirit of faith and of the love of God breathes in every page of our author's manuscript, and in this he is, we may well believe, the representative of those whose history he records. And it is this spirit which gives its Epic character to the history which he relates, for it is an Epic of the ways of God with men, of the vindication of His faithfulness to those who trust in Him.

The first foretaste of coming honour was when in 1630 the flowing tide of English

[1] This letter is printed at length at the end of this Essay.

emigration brought stronger and more promising Colonies to Salem and Boston, and the news was brought to our author that the instruction given to those who came out was "*that they should take advise of them at Plimoth, and should doe nothing to offend them;*" to which he appends the following characteristic note: "*Thus out of smalle beginings greater things have been prodused, by his hand y* made all things of nothing, and gives being to all things that are. And as one smalle candle may light a thousand so y* light here kindled hath shone unto many, yea in some sorte to our whole nation, let y* glorious name of Jehova have all y* praise.*" Bradford wrote his history at a time when Plymouth, having outlived the troubles and hardships of her early days, had become a strong and prosperous state with daughter Colonies around her, happy in the welfare of her people, honoured in the esteem of her neighbours, and a member of an organised confederacy of townships able to stand alone, supporting and supported by one another—the " United

Colonies of New England." And as he surveys the course of progress and growth by which out of weakness she has been made strong, he stands again in recollection with that forlorn band of Pilgrims who were landed, weather-beaten and homeless, upon an inhospitable shore, where *"which way so ever they turned their eys (save upward to y*^e* heavens), they could have little solace or content in respecte of any outward objects."* Before them an unknown, wintry country, behind them the mighty ocean *"to separate them from all y*^e* civill parts of y*^e* world. . . What could now sustain them, but y*^e* spirite of God and His Grace?"* Such was the first venture made in faith : and now *" May not & ought not the children of these fathers rightly say, our fathers were Englishmen which came over this great ocean and were ready to perish in this wilderness? But they cried unto y*^e* Lord, and He heard their voice, and looked on their adversitie ; let them therefore praise y*^e* Lord because He is good and His mercies endure for ever."*

A LETTER WRITTEN BY MR. ROBINSON
FROM LEYDEN TO THE COLONISTS
ON THE EVE OF THEIR DEPARTURE.

Loving & christian friends, I doe har-
tily & in y Lord salute you all, as being they
with whom I am presente in my best affection,
& most ernest longings after you, though I
be constrained for a while to be bodily absente
from you. I say constrained, God knowing how
willingly, & much rather then otherwise, I
would have borne my part with you in this
first brunt, were I not by strong necessitie held
back for y present. Make accounte of me in
y meanwhile, as of a man devided in my selfe
with great paine, and as (naturall bonds set a
side) having my beter parte with you. And
though I doubt not but in your godly wisdoms,
you both foresee & resolve upon y which con-
cerneth your presente state & condition both

D 2

severally and joyntly, yet have I thought it but my duty to add some further spur of provocation unto them, who rune already, If not because you need it, yet because I owe it in love & dutie.   And first, as we are daly to renew our repentance with our God, espetially for our sines known, and generally for our unknowne trespasses, so doth y Lord call us in a singuler manner upon occasions of shuch difficultie & danger as lieth upon you, to a both more narrow search, & careful reformation of your ways in his sight, least he calling to remembrance our sines forgotten by us or unrepented of, take advantage against us, & in judgmente leave us for y* same to be swalowed up in one danger or other; wheras on the contrary, sine being taken away by ernest repentance, & y* pardon therof from y* Lord sealed up unto a man's conscience by his Spirite, great shall be his securitie and peace in all dangers, sweete his comforts in all distreses, with hapie deliverance from all evill, whether in life or in death.*

Now next after this heavenly peace with

God & our owne consciences, we are carefully to provide for peace with all men what in us lieth, espetially with our associats, & for y^t watchfullnes must be had, that we neither at all in our selves doe give, no nor easily take offence being given by others. Woe be unto ye world for offences, for though it be necessarie (considering ye malice of Satan & man's corruption) that offences come, yet woe unto ye man or woman either by whom the offence cometh, saith Christ, Mat. 18. 7. And if offences in ye unseasonable use of things in themselves indifferent, be more to be feared then death itselfe, as ye Apostle teacheth, 1 Cor. 9. 15, how much more in things simply evill, in which neither honour of God nor love of man is thought worthy to be regarded. Neither yet is it sufficiente y^t we keepe ourselves, by ye grace of God, from giveing offence, excepte withall we be armed against ye taking of them when they be given by others. For how unperfect & lame is ye work of grace in y^t person, who wants charitie to cover a multitude of offences, as ye scriptures speaks.

Neither are you to be exhorted to this grace only upon y[e] comone grounds of christianitie, which are, that persons ready to take offence, either wante charitie, to cover offences, or wisdome duly to waigh humane frailtie, or lastly are grosse, though close hipocrites, as Christ our Lord teacheth, Mat. 7. 1, 2, 3; as indeed in my owne experience, few or none have bene found which sooner give offence, then shuch as easily take it; neither have they ever proved sound & profitable members in societies, which have nurished this touchey humor. But besids these, ther are diverse motives provoking you above others to great care & conscience this way: As first, you are many of you strangers, as to y[e] persons, so to y[e] Infirmities one of another, & so stand in neede of more watchfullnes this way, least when shuch things fall out in men & women as you suspected not, you be inordinatly affected with them; which doth require at your hands much wisdome & charitie for y[e] covering & preventing of incident offences that way. And lastly your intended course of civill comunitie will minister con-

*tinuall occasion of offence, & will be as fuell
for that fire, excepte you dilligently quench it
with brotherly forbearance. And if taking of
offence causlesly or easilie at men's doings be
so carefuly to be avoyded, how much more heed
is to be taken, y* we take not offence at God
himselfe, which yet we certainly doe so ofte as
we doe murmure at his providence in our
crosses, or beare impatiently shuch afflictions
as wherwith he pleaseth to visite us. Store
up therfore patience against y* evill day, without which we take offence at y* Lord himselfe
in his holy & just works.*

*A 4 thing ther is carfully to be provided
for, to witt, that with your comone imploy-
ments, you joyne commone affections truly bente
upon y* general good, avoyding as a deadly
plague of your both commone & severall com-
fort all retirednes of minde for proper advantage, and all singularly affected any maner of
way; let every man represe in himselfe & y*
whol body in each person, as so many rebels
against y* commone good, all private respects of
men's selves not sorting with y* general con-*

veniencie. And as men are carfull not to have a new house shaken with any violence before it be well setled & ye parts firmly knite; so be you, I beseech you, brethren, much more carfull, y^t the house of God which you are, and are to be, be not shaken with unnece-sarie novelties or other oppositions at ye first setling therof.

Lastly, wheras you are become a body politik, using amongst your selves civill gover-mente, and are not furnished with any persons of spetiall eminencie above ye rest, to be chosen by you, into office of goverment, Let your wisdome & godlines appeare, not only in chusing shuch persons as doe entirely love, and will promote ye comone good, but also in yeelding unto them all due honour, & obedi-ence in their lawfull administrations; not behoulding in them ye ordinarinesse of their persons, but Gods ordinance for your good; not being like ye foolish multitud, who more honour ye gay coate, then either ye vertuous minde of ye man, or glorious ordinance of ye Lord. But you know better things, & that *yᵉ image of yᵉ Lord's power & authoritie which yᵉ magistrate beareth, is honourable, in how meane persons so ever. And this dutie you both may yᵉ more willingly, and ought yᵉ more conscionably to performe because you are at least for yᵉ present to have only them for your ordinarie governours, which your selves shall make choyse of for that worke.*

Sundrie other things of importance I could put you in minde of, and of those before mentioned in more words, but I will not so farr wrong your godly minds, as to think you heedless of these things, ther being also diverce among you so well able to admonish both them selves & others of what concerneth them. These few things therfore, & yᵉ same in few words I doe ernestly commend unto your care, & conscience, joyning therwith my daily in- cessante prayers unto yᵉ Lord, yᵗ he who hath made yᵉ heavens & yᵉ earth, yᵉ sea and alᴌ rivers of waters, and whose providence is over all his workes, espetially over all his dear children for good, would so guide & gard you in your wayes, as inwardly by his Spirite, so outwardly by y⁴ hand of his power, as y⁴ both you & we allso, for & with you may have after matter of praising his name all y⁴ days of your and our lives. Fare you well in him in whom you trust, and in whom I rest.

An unfained well-wisher of your hapie success in this hopefull voyage.

John Robinson.

Note by Bradford.—" This letter though large, yet being so frutfull in it selfe, and suitable to their occation, I thought meete to inserte in this place."

NOTE—ON THE *MAYFLOWER*.

IT is curious how little the contemporary and early notices of the ship which brought over the first party of Pilgrims correspond with the celebrity to which that vessel has in these latter days attained. With us the *Mayflower* is a household word, a name of renown in two continents, she has a fame like that of the Argo in old classical Romance. But if we look at the old records, we find no such commemoration, but rather such a scarcity of evidence, as almost leaves room to doubt whether the ship was known by the name of the *May-flower* at all.

It is of course well known that mention of a ship *Mayflower* meets us at two separate periods in the records of the early Puritan Colonies of New England ; the earlier one being that which brought the first Pilgrims to Plymouth in 1620, the second that which made two journeys in 1629 and 1630, and brought over members of the two large parties which colonised Massachusetts Bay. Assuming that the earlier ship is rightly called the *Mayflower*, the further question arises, whether the former and the latter are the same.

It is a curious fact that of the first *Mayflower* there is extant no absolutely contemporary mention by name. It is of course not wonderful that the little band of exiles, seeking only a refuge where they would be left alone, should have been unconscious of the significance of their voyage, and of the interest which would afterwards attach to every detail connected with it. Those who make history are seldom aware of it at the time. It is not surprising that they should have taken no pains to inform the world of the name of their ship. But at the same time it is strange that no incidental allusion to the name of the vessel should occur, in the writings of either of the two passengers in her, who have left a record of their story behind

them. Yet such is the case. Bradford, whose history is the source from which most subsequent
writers have derived their information of the
migration, tells us everything else about the ship,
that she was a vessel of nine score tons, that she
was hired at London and was waiting for them
when they arrived at Southampton, and that her
master was Mr. Joans. He gives us all the details
of the starts and the puttings back, of the voyage,
of the delaying of the ship during the winter, of
her despatch homewards in March 1621. But
never once does he chance to mention her name nor
that of her consort, which brought them from
Holland and is generally known as the *Speedwell*.
They are to him always the "larger" and the
"lesser" ships, nor does Weston, of whose letter
the part relating to the return of the ship, and his
disappointment at her having no cargo, is quoted,
allude to her by name. And this is more remarkable because Bradford does mention the name of
the ship which arrived in the autumn of 1621, the
Fortune, and in the rest of his history we find that
nearly every other ship mentioned, is named either
by himself or by others in the course of correspondence. Bradford, moreover, tells us that some of the
second party from Leyden, in 1630, came in the
Mayflower. But he utters not a word of recognition
of an old friend, or of the coincidence of names.

There is another narrative of the early days of
the settlement at Plymouth, written by one of the
company, and even more detailed than Bradford's.
It is attributed to one G. Mourt, but is supposed to
embody the journal of Mr. E. Winslow. But in
this also no mention is made of the name of the
ship.

Captain John Smith, who more than once
mentions the voyage, and who seems familiar with
the details, the abandonment of the smaller ship,
the date of departure, &c., is similarly silent as to
the names. He does mention the *Mayflower* of
1629.

It is not till we come to Nathaniel Morton's
"*New England's Memorials*," published in 1669, that
we find the names we are seeking. He trans-
cribing, almost verbatim, Bradford's words, inserts
"*called the Speedwell*" "*called the Mayflower*," after
the first mention of the two ships respectively. And
he repeats the name of the *Mayflower* in recording
her final departure from England. It is curious
that he shows no knowledge of the second
Mayflower that brought the remainder of the
Leyden party in 1630.

Cotton Mather in his "*Magnalia*" takes up
Morton's version, and speaks of them as the
Speedwell and the *Mayflower*.

But Mr. Thomas Prince, who published in

1736 his "*New England Chronology*," for which he tells us he borrowed the greatest part of his intelligence from his much honoured uncle William Bradford, and such MSS. as he left in his study relating to the years 1620–1646, has no knowledge of the first *Mayflower*. He mentions the second *Mayflower* without a word of recognition, and this is the more remarkable as he is interested in the previous history of another ship, viz. the *Arabella* of which he records, on the authority of Mr. Johnson, that she had before been called the *Eagle*. The fact that he was interested in the former history of the one, renders it more unlikely that a far more interesting fact in the former history of the other would have escaped him if it were a fact.

We find therefore that we are brought to Nathaniel Morton as the authority on which the ascription to the first ship of the name of *Mayflower* depends. He came to Plymouth in 1623, being then eleven years old, and perhaps it would be hypercritical to question the accuracy of his information. We may accept his statement, though we cannot but be struck by the curious omission on the part of those from whom we might have expected at any rate a casual mention.

But when we come to the question of the identity of the first *Mayflower* with the second, the evidence seems more than doubtful. We know from the records of the Massachusetts Bay Company that the *Mayflower* formed part of the little fleet which took out Higginson's Company to Salem in 1629. She was a ship of Yarmouth, her master Mr. Pierce. Higginson in his journal mentions all his ships, with the tonnage and equipment of ordnance of all the others. But unfortunately, of the *Mayflower* he only says that she carried provisions and passengers.

Governor Winthrop also records the names of all his eleven ships, the *Mayflower* among them. She left Southampton in May 1630, and arrived at Charleston on July 1, which nearly corresponds with the date given by Bradford for the arrival of the second batch of the Leyden party. But none of these contemporary writers give any hint that this *Mayflower* of Yarmouth was the same as that which nine years before had been hired at London.

It is not till we come to Savage, who, in 1825, reprinted Winthrop's works, and to Young, who quotes the records of the company, and Higginson's journal, above referred to, in his "*Chronicles*," published in 1841 and 1846, that we meet with the confident assertion that the former and the latter *Mayflower* were the same. But they bring no evidence beyond their own word. In view, therefore, that *Mayflower* was a common name, borne doubtless by ships from many ports, and in the absence of further evidence that might naturally be expected, we submit that the identity of the *Mayflower* hired in London with the *Mayflower* of Yarmouth nine years later remains unproven.

II

THE COLONISATION OF NEW PLYMOUTH
—HOW IT WAS PROMOTED AND
FINANCED.

THE migration of the Pilgrim Fathers was
essentially a religious movement, the action
of men who forsook home and kindred for
what they conceived to be the only true
principles of their Lord, and who were ready
to "*goe into a cuntrie they knew not (but by
hearsay), an adventure almost desperate, a
case intolerable and a miserie worse than death
—for their desires were sett on the ways of
God, and to enjoye his ordinances*" and "*they
rested on his providence, and knew whom they
had beleeved.*" But a resolution like this, however spiritual in its origin and motive, must
take a practical shape and must issue on its
material side in an undertaking subject to the

E

same conditions and necessities as those of ordinary life. And the proposed migration to New England, involving a voyage which then lasted several weeks, and the necessity to provide also for the first winter in their new home, was an undertaking of considerable magnitude. Even Pilgrims have bodies to be transported and mouths to be filled. It became in fact, on its mundane side, a colonial adventure, to be provided for and conducted after the manner then usual with such undertakings.

It was not left to the Pilgrims to discover for themselves the way in which their Colony must be formed. There had been others in the field before them. The age which succeeded that of Elizabeth was an age in which that glamour of adventure and imagination, which invested the exploits of the first discoverers, was wearing off, and men were settling down soberly to appraise the worth of what they had gained, and the best way of turning it to account. Colonisation was being taken up as a serious business by men who recognised that the promise of the New

World lay not in dreams of fabulous gold mines, and rich prizes of Spanish galleons, but in the hard-won profits of trade and cultivation, the fruits of honest work. "*There is no country to pillage as the Romans found*," wrote Captain John Smith of his Colony of Virginia; "*all you must expect from thence must be by labour.*"

As a consequence of this business-like spirit, the principles of colonisation had already been reduced to system. And the system adopted was that which has played a very large part, for good or ill, in the history of British colonisation. It was in fact the system of what we should now call a Chartered Company. The first promoters of such an undertaking were men of position and substance, such as Sir Ferdinando Gorges, whose name is often met with in the pages of Bradford's narrative, Lord Chief Justice Popham, the Earl of Warwick, Lord Saye and Sele, and other prominent persons. These formed a council to project the Colony, and provide for its general administration,

They then proceeded to obtain a Royal
Patent or Charter, guaranteeing to them the
exclusive right of settlement and trade within
the specified area, with other clearly defined
powers of government. Thus there was
already a Virginia Company incorporated
in 1606, whose Patent originally included
the whole of New England, as well as
Virginia proper, to which their occupation
was in fact confined. And when the resolution to migrate to North America[1] was
finally taken by the Leyden Pilgrims, it was
to the Virginia Company that they first had
recourse, with the idea of forming a distinct
body, to live by themselves, but under the
general government of Virginia. What
was wanted was another Patent, or sub-lease,
under the Company whereby the privileges
granted to the general Company as a whole
were transmitted to themselves, so far as the

[1] The alternative suggestion was to choose *Guiana* as a
residence, and there is, at the present time, a special interest
in the reason alleged as an inducement thereto, that *the
Spaniards (haveing much more than they could possess) had
not yet planted there, nor any where very near ye same.*—
Bradford M.S., p. 18.

limited area assigned to them was concerned.
It would secure for them the right of occupation and trade, to the exclusion of intruders
from outside, leaving them independence in
their local self-government, while it incorporated them under the general government and protection of Virginia, as a
dependency of the British Crown. In the
unsettled state of the country, however, this
general government and protection was
likely, at first, to be more of a name than a
reality.

Such a Patent was applied for, and at
length, after considerable trouble, was granted.
The negotiations which took place were
complicated by the pursuit of another object,
the granting of which did not rest with the
Company, but for which appeal had to be
made directly to the King, through the Privy
Council. What they desired was the right
of freedom of religion, that is exemption
from the authority of the National Church,
which was obligatory upon all British subjects
within the King's dominions, and which they

had had to flee to Holland to escape. It
was hoped that the King would give them such
a licence of freedom, confirmed under the
Broad Seal, and they had "*some great persons
of good rank and qualitie*," whose influence
would be used on their behalf. This, however, could not be effected. The influence of
the Archbishop was against them. However,
they "*prevailed so far in sounding his
Majestie's mind, that he would connive at them
and not molest them so long as they carried
themselves peacably ;*" but confirmation under
the Broad Seal was not to be expected. It
was a disappointment, but they comforted
themselves with the shrewd reflection that
"*though they had a seale as broad as the
houseflore*" it would be no real protection, if
there should be a desire at any time to revoke
it. This desired independence in religion
formed no part of the Patent of the Company,
though many of their friends in the Company
exerted themselves to procure it for them.

The Patent, obtained with great pains
and delay, from the Virginia Company was,

however, never used. While they were engaged in negotiations for the means of transport, and making their preparations, there came to them at Leyden a Mr. Weston, who was the principal agent of the capitalists with whom they were in treaty, and he told them that "*sundrie Honble Lords had obtained a large grante from ye King for ye more northerly parts of that countrie derived out of the Virginia patente, and wholy secluded from their govermente, and to be called by another name, viz. New England.*" And he advised them to turn their thoughts in this direction.

What he referred to was the revival of a branch of the Virginia Company, which had originally been incorporated as far back as 1606 under the name of the Plymouth [1] or North Virginia Company, and which had recently been re-established by the efforts

---

[1] Called "*Plymouth*" because the Patent was originally granted for Plymouth and the western counties of England. This name "*New England*" was substituted for that of North Virginia by Captain John Smith after his exploration in 1614.

of Sir Ferdinando Gorges and others, with
the title of the New England Company.
A book is extant, of which a copy is in the
British Museum, entitled "*A briefe relation
of the discovery and plantation of New
England*," set forth in 1622 by the President
and Council of New England. It consists of
a kind of Manifesto of the said Council,
giving an account of several attempts which
had been made in previous years to plant
Colonies, though without success, and taking
credit for having collected much information,
which has prepared the way for future
Colonists. It sets forth a scheme of government for the prospective Colony under a
Governor General, Treasurer, "*Martial*,"
Admiral and other functionaries, and further
provides for the division of the country into
Baronis, Manors, &c. The present object
of the Council is to obtain a fresh Patent,
and to invite would-be Colonists to join in a
community, or joint stock together. Bradford alludes to this book by its full title, but
without much respect. And though he does

not say that it was under this company that
the Plymouth Colony were to obtain their
Patent, yet such must have been the case.[1]
As a matter of fact, indeed, owing partly to
the shortness of the time before the migration, partly also, doubtless, to the fact that
this company did not obtain its new Patent
till November 1620, the Pilgrim Fathers had
to sail without a Patent. And this lack of
legal authorisation gave occasion for an outbreak of discontent, and the expression of
mutinous intentions on the part of some of
the Colonists on their arrival at Cape Cod.
The hardships of the voyage, and the gloomy
outlook of the new country, seem to have
relaxed the bonds of loyalty. And these mal-
contents avowed that in the absence of a
charter nobody had a right to command
them, and they would use their liberty. The

[1] The "*Briefe Relation*" concludes with a bare allusion to
the fact that the Company has "*a peaceable plantation at this
present* (1622) *among them* (*the Indians*), *where our people
both prosper and live in good liking and assuredness of their
neighbours,*" which seems to be a reference to the Plymouth
Colony.

lack of legal sanction, however, was remedied
for the time by a bond [1] of mutual combination
in fidelity to one another, and in allegiance
to the King, which was signed by all the
company on board the ship before dis-
embarking. And a Patent was obtained
afterwards, of which information was sent by
the next ship, which came out in the following
autumn : " *we have procured you a charter, the
best we could, which is better than your former,*

---

[1] This " Acte" is very interesting ; it ran as follows :—

*In y[e] name of God Amen. We whose names are under-
writen, the loyall subjects of our dread soveraigne Lord King
James by y[e] grace of God, of great Britaine, Franc, & Ireland
king, defender of y[e] faith, &c.*

*Haveing undertaken, for y[e] glorie of God, and advance-
mente of y[e] christian faith and honour of our king & countrie,
a voyage to plant y[e] first colonie in y[e] Northerne parts of
Virginia, doe by these presents solemnly and mutualy in y[e]
presence of God, and one of another, covenant, & combine our
selves togeather into a civill body politick; for our better
ordering, & preservation & furtherance of y[e] ends aforesaid ;
and by vertue hearof to enacte, constitute, and frame shuch just
& equall lawes, ordinances, Acts, constitutions, & offices,
from time to time, as shall be thought most meete & convenient
for y[e] generall good of y[e] colonie : unto which we promise all
due submission and obedience. In witnes wherof we have
hereunder subscribed our names at Cap Codd y[e] 11 of November, in y[e] year of y[e] raigne of our soveraigne Lord King
James of England, France, & Ireland y[e] eighteenth, and of
Scotland y[e] fiftie-fourth. An[o] dom. 1620.*

and with less limitation."[1] The establishment
of the Colony was thus complete so far as
legal sanction was concerned.

Before passing from this subject, a few
passages of interest in respect of this and
other Patents, and their bearing upon the
history of Plymouth, may be briefly glanced
at. It appears that the Patent was first
taken, "*by reason of acquaintance,*" in the
name of Mr. Pierce, one of the leading
Adventurers. It was of course understood
that he took it in trust for the rest. But
when he saw that the prospects of the Colony
looked hopeful, and had won the favour of
the New England Council, he applied for
and obtained another Patent of much larger
extent, apparently on behalf of the Colony,
though in his own name. But his design
was "*to keep it to himselfe, and alow them
what he pleased, to hold of him as tenants,*

[1] The "*less limitation*" probably refers to the provisions
as to religion. The New England Company was founded
on more liberal principles as to religion than that of Virginia, and the Colonists may have received that sanction for
religious freedom which they desired.

and sue to his courts as cheefe lord." It
appears to have been a discreditable transac-
tion, and would have secured for him
formidable rights over the rising plantation.
Pierce was accused of breach of trust by
other members of the company, and forced
to part with his "*royall lordship.*" He
succeeded in exacting, however, a price of
500*l.* for that, "*which cost him but* 50*l.*," and
then further sued the company in most of the
chief courts in England, and even brought it
to Parliament. He fitted out a ship called the
Paragon with goods for the Colony, and the
fact that this ship was twice driven back by
unusually severe weather was taken for a
sign that "*the hand of God was justly
against him.*" "*But,*" says Bradford, "*he is
now dead and I will leave him to* y*ᵉ Lord.*"

The question of a Patent arose again
when the company of Adventurers broke
up and was succeeded by the partnership of
the eight "undertakers." Application was
made just at the time that the Massachusetts
Company were projecting their great settle-

ment in Boston Bay, and had obtained their
unusually large powers—a fact which stirred
the friends of Plymouth to emulation. The
following letter written by Mr. Sherley, one
of the partners, is a very interesting
specimen of business correspondence, which
was then not always carried on with that
excessive economy of ideas and words which
now prevails. The writer is somewhat of a
gossip, and moralises, with a scriptural
allusion more ingenious than accurate, upon
the trite subject of the venality of men in
office. But the style is characteristic, the
picture of underhand influences is probably
not untrue, and the remarks about the Patent
are noteworthy.

Most worthy and loving freinds,—
Some of your letters I received in July, &
some since by Mr. Peirce, but till our maine
bussines ye patent was granted, I could not
setle my mind, nor pen to writing. Mr.
Allerton was so turmoyled about it, as verily
I would not, nor could not have undergone it,

*if I might have had a thousand pounds; but y*ᵉ *Lord so blessed his labours, (even beyond ex-pectation in these evill days), as he obtained y*ᵉ *love & favors of great men in repute, & place. He got granted from y*ᵉ *Earle of War-wick, & s*ʳ *Fferdinando Gorge, all that Mr. Winslow desired in his letters, to me, & more allso, which I leave to him to relate. Then he sued to y*ᵉ *king, to confirme their grante, and to make you a corporation, and so to inable you to make, & execute lawes, in such large, & ample maner, as y*ᵉ *Massa-chusett plantation hath it. Which y*ᵉ *king graciously granted; referring it to y*ᵉ *Lord keeper, to give order to y*ᵉ *solisiter to draw it up, if ther were a presidente for it. So ye Lord keeper furthered it all he could, and allso y*ᵉ *solisiter (but as Festus* [!] *said to Paule, with no small sume of money obtained I this freedom); for by y*ᵉ *way many ridells must be resolved, and many locks must be opened with y*ᵉ *silver, ney y*ᵉ *golden key. Then it was to come to y*ᵉ *lord Treasurer, to have his war-rente, for freeing y*ᵉ *custume for a certain*

*time ; but he would not doe it, but refferd it
to y[e] counsell table. And ther Mr. Allerton
atended day by day, when they satte, but could
not gett his petition read. And by reason of
Mr. Peirce his staying, with all y[e] passengers
at Bristoll, he was forct to leave y[e] further
prosecuting of it, to a solissiter. But ther is
no fear, nor doubte but it will be granted, for
he hath y[e] cheefe of them to freind, yet it will
be marvelouly needfull for him to returne by
y[e] first ship y[t] comes from thence ; for if you
had this confirmed, then were you compleate,
and might bear such sway, & goverment, as
were fitt for your ranke, & place y[t] God hath
called you unto. And stope y[e] moueths, of
base and scurrulous fellowes, y[t] are ready to
question, & threaten you in every action you
doe, &c.*

It was dated March 19, 1629.[1]

The Patent upon which money was thus

---

[1] Mr. Thomas Prince, who used the " *Bradford M.S.*" for
his " *New England Chronology*" (published in 1736), and who
has made some annotations in the blank pages, remarks here
that the letter is dated according to the Old Style, which
reckoned the year 1629 as lasting till March 25, 1630.

spent was never obtained. Mr. Allerton,
the agent of the partners, left it unfinished,
because he wanted, for private ends, to come
back to England, and the opportunity lost
did not occur again. We do not find, however, that the want of it was much felt by the
Colony. But a Patent must have been
obtained at some time, and taken out in the
name of Bradford and his heirs, for we find
it recorded,—and it is an incident which
comes in with singularly dramatic propriety ·
towards the end of his narrative, if not of his
public career,—that in the year 1640, in consequence of the growth of the Colony and the
expansion of Plymouth into now nine
flourishing townships, William Bradford for
himself, his heirs and assigns did formally
surrender his Patent, and resign into the
hands of the people the rights and powers
he had had on their behalf, and which by his
faithful stewardship they were now in a condition to exercise themselves.

But the subject of the Patent has occupied
us too long. The Colonists when meditating

emigration had to face the further and more pressing question of finance. When they left England in 1607–8 they were men in humble life, "*not acquainted with trads nor traffique . . . but had only been used to a plain countrie life and ye inocente trade of husbandrey.*" The stay in Holland had not improved their circumstances, for it was "*the grimme and grisly face of povertie coming upon them like an armed man*" that forced them to remove. How was the capital to be found to provide them with ships for transport and supplies for their sustenance and trade, not only during the voyage, but also during the first months, perhaps years, of their settlement? After a good deal of negotiation, lasting more than two years, the agents sent over from Leyden Mr. John Carver, and Mr. Robert Cushman found means to engage with a company of Adventurers or speculators, of whom the above-mentioned Mr. Weston was among the chief, to form a joint stock corporation for the purpose. It was formed on the basis

F

of 10*l.* shares. Every person, above 16, adventuring his person was rated as holder of a single share; if he further furnished himself with 10*l.* worth of equipment, his share was double. Between the ages of ten and sixteen two persons represented a share. Of those who came later and who died earlier, the shares were reckoned proportionately. Those who adventured only their money, had a share for every 10*l.* so invested. The partnership was to last for seven years, (unless otherwise terminated by the whole company), during which time all the profits were to accumulate; and at the end of that time "*y*ͤ *capitall and profits, viz. the houses, lands, goods, and chatles,*" were to be divided amongst the shareholders. All the members of the Colony were during the seven years to work for "*the general,*" and to have their meat and drink, apparel and all provisions out of the common stock.

These terms were very hard, and the Colonists pleaded that their agent, Mr. Cushman, had without authority deviated from the terms they had originally drafted, which differed in two respects, viz. (1) that the houses, and cultivated lands, especially the gardens, were to be excepted from the general division, remaining the property of the planters, and (2) that these were to have two days in the week for their own private employment. "*The land and house*," writes Mr. Robinson pathetically to Mr. Carver, "*will be but a trifell for advantage to y*ᵉ *adventurers, and yet the devision of it a great discouragemente to y*ᵉ *planters, who would with singuler care make it comfortable with borrowed houres from their sleep.*" And again, "*consider also how much unfite that you and your like must serve a new prentiship of 7 years, and not a daies freedom from taske.*" A good deal of tart recrimination passed between the Leyden party and their agent Mr. Cushman, but the latter protested that the Adventurers would not hear of any change, that the first mention of it had caused one of them at once to withdraw 500*l*., and that if they refused the

F 2

terms the whole project would be "*dasht.*"
The Colonists still refused consent, and the
agreement was unsigned when they sailed,
but they yielded to Weston's pressure and
signed it in the following year.

The scheme was harsh and impolitic.   It
verified one of Bradford's proverbs, "*covetous-
ness never brings ought home.*"   The Colonists,
bound by a yoke of bondage to the Adventurers, had little heart for their work.   They
were inclined to rely too much on the
supplies to be sent from home.   Wanting
the spring of private enterprise, they failed
to do their utmost for themselves.   It might
have been expected that the early months of
the first year, while waiting for harvest,
would be a time of scarcity.   But though
that harvest brought a temporary plenty, yet
the second spring was even worse than the
first.   The community had to be placed on
famine rations of $\frac{1}{4}$ lb. of bread per head ; the
morale of the Colony showed signs of break-
ing down, and thefts of corn became of daily
occurrence.   The Communistic system had

to be relaxed, at least so far as to allow every family a temporary holding of a "*parcell of land according to the proportion of their numbers*," to sow corn, so as to throw them on their own resources. There was no more famine after this. But it was not only the economical grievance that harassed the Colonists. There was also the further consequence of this bondage, that the liberty which they prized so highly, liberty as a church and as a community, was undermined. They were subject to the control of the Adventurers in things which touched their dearest principles. They had to accept as fellow-settlers whomsoever the Adventurers chose to send, however undesirable in respect either of religious sympathies or of general character. And this hardship was aggravated by the self-seeking of some of the Adventurers, who tried to push their own private advantage in violation of the principles of partnership, which secured the monopoly of the trade to the company. We have glanced at the conduct of Mr. Pierce. Mr.

Weston, in spite of vehement promises of
perpetual support, openly broke off from the
company that he might, (though he failed
ignominiously), trade on his own account,
to the injury of "*the general.*" Moreover
the second ship which came out from the
company at home, the *Anne*, brought 50
people, many of whom were so incapable
that the Colony had to bear the expense of
sending them home again. She brought out
also the ominous accession of "*a company
that did not belong to y*ᵉ *general body, but
came one their perticuler, and were to have
lands assigned them, and be for themselves, and
yet to be subjecte to y*ᵉ *generall goverment.*"
The seeds of disintegration were thus sown.
Accommodation had to be made for these
"particulars," within the Colony hitherto
united in oneness of interest and organisation.
The next year some of the company de-
manded leave to join the Particulars, and their
demand had to be granted. The rise and
growth of discordant interests in the little
body which numbered under 200 people went

on apace. The assignment of an acre of land to every person in permanent possession was a salutary measure, but insufficient. Disagreement arose in a new form. That summer the Adventurers sent out as a preacher a Mr. Lyford, apparently a disgraced clergyman of the Church of England, and after a little while he and a *"particular"* named Mr. Oldham formed a faction, which led to grave disorders and violent measures. Lyford and Oldham appealed home, where other rumours injurious to the Colony had already been received. And the Adventurers wrote to express dissatisfaction. The nature of these objections is summarised by Bradford with the answers, in a paper which contains many points of interest, besides its amusing unconventionality.

I shall here set them (the objections) downe, with y^e* answers then made unto them, and sent over at y*^e* returne of this ship: Which did so confound y*^e* objecters; As some confessed their falte, and others deneyed what they* *had said, and eate their words, & some others of them, have since come over againe, and here lived to convince themselves sufficiently, both in their owne, & other men's judgments.*

1. obj. was diversitie aboute religion.

Ans. : we know no shuch matter, for here was never any controversie, or opposition, either publicke, or private (to our knowledg) since we came.

2. ob. : Neglecte of familie duties, one ye Lord's day.

Ans. We allow no such thing, but blame it in our selves, & others ; and they that thus reporte it, should have shewed their christian love the more, if they had in love tould ye offenders of it ; rather then thus to reproach them behind their baks. But (to say no more) we wish them selves had given better example.

3. ob. Wante of both the sacrements.

Ans. The more is our greefe, that our pastor is kept from us, by whom we might injoye them ; for we used to have the Lords supper, every saboth ; and baptisme as often as ther was occasion of children to baptise.

4. *ob. Children not catachised, nor taught to read.*

Ans. : neither is true; for diverse take pains with their owne as they can. Indeed we have no commone schoole for want of a fit person, or hithertoo means to maintaine one ; though we desire now to begine.

5. *ob. Many of ye perticuler members of ye plantation will not work for ye generall.*

Ans. : this allso is not wholy true ; for though some doe it not willingly, & other not honestly, yet all doe it ; and he that doth worst gets his owne foode, & something besids. But we will not excuse them, but labour to reforme them ye best we cane; or else to quitte ye plantation of them.

6. *ob. : The water is not wholsome.*

Ans. : If they mean, not so wholsome as ye good beere and wine in London, (which they so dearly love,) we will not dispute with them, but els for water it is as good as any in ye world (for ought we knowe), and it is wholsome enough to us, that can be contente therwith.

7. *ob.* *The ground is barren, and doth bear no grasse.*

Ans.: It is heer (as in all places) some better, & some worse; and if they well consider their woods in England, they shall not find shuch grasse in them, as in their feelds, & meadows. The cattle find grasse, for they are as fatt as need be; we wish we had but one for every hundred, that here is grase to keep. Indeed this objection (as some other) are ridiculous to all here which see, and know ye contrary.

8 *ob.: The fish will not take salt to keepe sweete.*

Ans.: This is as true, as that which was written, that ther is scarce a foule to be seene, or a fish to be taken. Things likly to be true in a cuntrie, wher so many sayle of ships come yearly a-fishing; they might as well say, ther can no aile, or beere in London, be kept from sowering.

9 *ob.: Many of them are theevish, and steale on from an other.*

Ans.: Would London had been free from

that crime; then we should not have been trobled with these here; It is well knowne sundrie have smarted well for it, and so are ye rest like to doe, if they be taken.

10 ob.: The cuntrie is anoyed with foxes, and woules.

Ans.: So are many other good cuntries too; but poyson, Traps, and other such means will help to destroy them.

11 ob.: The Dutch are planted nere Hudsons Bay, and are likly to overthrow the trade.

Ans.: They will come and plante in these parts also, if we and others doe not, but goe home and leave it to them. We rather commend them, then condemne them for it.

12 ob.: The people are much anoyed with muskeetoes.

Ans.: They are too delicate, and unfitte to begine new-plantations, and collonies that cannot enduer ye biting of a muskeeto; we would wish such to keepe at home, till at least they be muskeeto proofe, yet this place is as free as any, and experience teacheth that y^f

more ye land is tild, and ye woods cut downe,
the fewer ther will be, and in the end scarce
any at all.

The episode of Oldham and Lyford is
full of the liveliest interest, and though it
must be remembered that we have but one
side of the story, yet we can hardly doubt
that the measures taken with them were
necessary for the very existence of the Colony.
The result was, however, that "*the Company
of adventurers broake in peeces here upon.*"
There were amongst them some who were
dissatisfied with the Colonists and out of
sympathy with their religious views. These
wrote complaining that the Plymouth Church
had incurred the name of "*Brownists*," and
requiring as a condition of continuing in partnership that London influence should be para-
mount in the government, as in the trade of
the Colony; that the "*French discipline*"
should be *ex animo* adopted; and that Mr.
Robinson and those who, with him, were
waiting at Leyden for a chance of coming

over should not be allowed to do so unless they were reconciled to "*our Church*" by a recantation.

That party among the Adventurers who favoured the Colonists, wrote in a more friendly strain, though, as a practical comment upon their words, they sent goods for which they exacted prices at the rate of 70 per cent. And then the end of the joint stock company soon came. The Colony bought the interest of the home company for 1,800*l*., to be paid in instalments, and a general division of lands and goods was made among the whole community. Then a partnership was formed between Bradford and three others on the Plymouth side, and three partners, afterwards increased to four, in London, who hired the trade of the Colony for six years, on condition of paying the 1,800*l*. and all debts. And so it came about that the Colony, emancipated from a harsh and alien control, was enabled to work out its development in freedom. There were difficulties arising from the weakness, with which the London partners allowed themselves to be used by their clever but unscrupulous agent, named Allerton, to prosecute schemes injurious to the common interests; and an interminable correspondence arose over a ship called the *White Angel*. But this did not interrupt the flow of the now rising tide of prosperity. The first use of their freedom made by Bradford and his colleagues was to send for their friends, at Leyden, who were brought in the *Talbot* and *Mayflower* to MassachusettsBay in 1629 and 1630, and were fetched from thence to Plymouth. And the results did not end there. It was to this brave venture on the part of her second governor and his friends, that Plymouth owed her extrication from difficulties which might have strangled her in her infancy, and her establishment in a position of honour and usefulness in the world.

A few words in conclusion as to the subsequent relations of the Colony with the New England Company, and the Home Government. In the June of 1623 a ship came out bringing a Captain Francis West, who had a

commission to be Admiral of New England,
to restrain interlopers, and such ships as came
to fish and trade without a licence from the
Council. But, says Bradford, "*he could doe
no good of them for they were to stronge for
him. And he found ye fishermen to be stuborne
fellows.*" He went away to Virginia, and
shortly after this fishing was made free by
Parliament.

In the September of the same year Captain
Robert Gorges, son of Sir Ferdinando, came to
Massachusetts Bay bearing a commission from
the Council as Governor General of New England. He was to form a Council consisting
of the aforesaid Admiral, a Mr. Christopher
Levite, the Governor for the time being of
Plymouth, and such others as he approved.
And he with his Council, or any two of them,
had authority to do and execute what to them
should seem good in all cases, capital,
criminal, and civil. Thus the authority conveyed to the Company by Patent was of the
fullest. But neither in this, nor in any other
instance in Bradford's time was it ever

seriously put into effect. Captain Gorges did indeed call Weston to account, with sundry threatenings, which came to nothing. But he was more intent on planting a Colony on his own account, in a territory granted to him in Boston Bay. And his public functions, as did these private operations also, soon came to nothing. When in 1628 Morton's excesses became a source of danger to his neighbours, it was to Plymouth, and to no publicly constituted authority, that they applied for assistance. The New England Colonies were left to make their way by themselves without the protection, and consequently in independence, of the home authorities. In 1635 Mr. Winslow was instructed while in England to appeal to the Privy Council to take some measures against the encroachments of the French and Dutch. But nothing was done, and the Privy Council soon had other work to attend to in the troubles which were arising at home. The New England Colonies, forced thus to shift for themselves, formed a Confederacy for their own protection and support, and in the preamble to the Articles of Confederation they stated as one of the reasons for such combination, that by reason of the distractions in England "*we are hindered from ye humble way of seeking advice, or reaping those comfortable fruits of protection, which at other times we might well expect.*" Thus the waves of great civil struggles in England were felt on the further shores of the Atlantic, and produced results of far-reaching consequence not only to the Colonies themselves, but to the World. The young communities which were springing up in all the vigour of youth in this new Country were doubtless soon quite able to take care of themselves, and by no means inclined to submit to control. But it was assuredly to the circumstance of their being thus left alone that we must attribute much of that rapid development of self-reliance and independence, which have borne their fruit in the great Republic of the West.

III

GLIMPSES OF THE LAND AND OF THE TIMES

" *Then* " (after passing Quonahassit south-wards) " *we come to Accomack an excellent good harbor, good land: and no want of anything but industrious people. After much kindness; upon a small occasion wee fought also with fortie or fiftie of those; though some were hurt, and some were slaine; yet within an hour after they became friends. Cape Cod is the next that presents itself, which is only a headland of high hils of sand overgrowne with shrubbie pines, hurts and such trash: but an excellent harbor for all weathers. This cape is made by the maine sea on the one side, and a great Bay on the other in forme of a sickle: on it doth inhabit the people of Pawmet; and in the bottom of the Bay the people of Chawum.*"

These are the words[1] of the man who first discovered the capabilities of the site of New Plymouth for colonisation. Captain John Smith, one of the most adventurous and practical of English explorers in North America, finding himself in the spring of 1614 off the coast of North Virginia, as it was then called, and at leisure, while the rest of his company were fishing, took eight men in an open boat, and spent eighty days in exploring the great bay which extends from Penobscot to Cape Cod. The results of his investigation he published on his return, with a map of the coast. And to him belongs the honour of having discerned, and first called attention to, the qualities which were afterwards to make New England the most promising field for English colonisation. In the course of exploration he not only made acquaintance with the coast-line, but also informed himself of the names given by the natives, and in some cases by fishermen, to

[1] In the *Description of New England*, first published (with the map, of which a facsimile is given in this volume) in 1616. See Arber's Reprint, p. 205.

places on the shore. Among these was Accomack. On returning to England he tells us
that he submitted the map of his discoveries
to Prince Charles (afterwards Charles I.),
with the request that he would become god-
father to the country by giving it new
names. The map as it is presented to our
readers is the result : and it reveals the
interesting fact, that Plymouth had already
received its name four years before the
arrival of the Pilgrim Fathers. Smith
appends a table on which a list of some
thirty-two old and new names are set
forth in parallel columns, among them
Accomack, newly called Plimouth. One
point of interest about these names is that
which he probably least anticipated, viz.
that, in spite of this princely sanction, the
greater number of them never took root. Subsequent occupiers of the territory used their
own discretion as to the names they adopted.
And so there is ground for Nath. Morton's
statement, that the name of Plimouth was so
called, not only for the reason above men-

tioned, "*but also because Plimouth in Old England was the last town they left in their native country, and for that they received many kindnesses from some Christians there.*"

Bradford was, however, acquainted with this previous name, and quotes a letter written by Mr. Dermer, a former associate of Capt. John Smith, which introduces many points of interest.

This Mr Dermer was hear the same year that these people[1] *came, as apears by a relation writen by him, & given me by a freind. Bearing date June 30. An°. 1620. And they*[1] *came in Novemb^r following, so ther was but 4 months difference. In which relation to his Honrd friend, he hath these pasages of this very place.*

I will first begine (saith he) with that place from whence Squanto, or Tisquantem, was taken away : wh. in cap. Smiths mape is called Plimoth : and I would that Plimoth had

---

[1] Bradford habitually alludes to his fellow-colonists as "these people" or "they," a fact which leads to some ambiguity in his narrative at times.

ye like comodities. I would that the first plantation might hear be seated, if ther come to the number of 50 persons, or upward. Otherwise at Charlton, because ther ye savages are lese to be feared. The Pocanawkits which live to ye west of Plimoth, bear an invetrate malice to ye English, and are of more streingth then all ye savags from thence to Penobscote. Their desire of revenge was occasioned by an English man, who having many of them on bord, made a great slaughter with their murderers, & smale shot, when as (they say) they offered no injurie on their parts.

One thing that strikes us in this letter is that Capt. Smith's map is referred to, as early as 1620, as the recognised authority, at the time, on the geography of New England. It represents all that was known by the world at large on the configuration of the country. It is very remarkable, and at the same time highly creditable to the worthy Captain, that in the short space of eighty days, and with the very limited resources he possessed, he should have succeeded in making a map so careful and accurate, at least in its general outlines. But at the same time the fact that it presented only the coast-line, and could not pretend to give internal features, or to trace the course of rivers beyond their mouths, bore curious results in after years. In the years 1639 and 1640 a dispute arose between the townships of Hingam and Sityate as to their boundaries, which involved further issues as to the territory of Plymouth and Massachusetts. The cause of the dispute was that the Patent originally granted to Hingam provided "*that from Charles-river or any branch or part thereof they were to extend their limits and three myles further to y*ᵉ* Southward.*" On the authority of this grant the people of Hingam, finding "*a smale river or brooke rather, that a great way within land trended southward and issued into some part of y*ᵉ* river taken to be Charles River,*" and taking a point three miles southward of the extremity of this brook, drew a line eastward to the

sea.   This line of demarcation was highly
advantageous to the men of Hingam, and
was equally objectionable to Sityate and
Plymouth, for it included a territory which
took in not only all the surroundings of
Sityate, but reached even to a part of Plymouth itself.   The dispute was conducted
with much warmth and some violence.
The one party planted their stakes in the
coveted meadow grounds, which stakes the
others promptly pulled up.   Recourse was
had ultimately to arbitration, and Capt.
Smith's map was called in evidence.   It was
urged that Charles River, as named in that
map, could no more be taken to include
every little brook that ultimately found issue
through it to the sea, than the Humber in
Old England included the Trent and Ouse
and all the smaller rivers and brooks that fell
into them.   And in the end the arbitration
resulted in a formal delimitation of boundaries, in favour of Sityate, the landmarks
of which, such as Bound Brook and Great
Pond, are recognised to the present day.

But to return to the point at which the Pilgrim Fathers first set foot on the *terra firma* of Cape Cod and Accomack, described above by Capt. Smith and Mr. Dermer. It was a land as yet uncolonised. To the north there was an English settlement at Newfoundland and a fishing-station at Monahigan. The French were settled at Nova Scotia, and were extending their influence towards Penobscot. To the south the Dutch were planting themselves at Manhattan, afterwards New York ; and further south still was the far from prosperous English Colony of Virginia. The description of Accomack given by Dermer might well arouse those apprehensions which had troubled the minds of the Pilgrims while still at Leyden. To their disquieted imaginations it appeared to some that they were going to utter ruin. Besides the chances of famine and nakedness, of unwholesome diet, air, and water, there was unknown peril of savage enemies, people who were cruel, barbarous, treacherous, and merciless. The savages whom they might

expect to meet would practise every refinement of cruelty, "*fleaing some alive with
ye shells of fishes, cutting of ye members and
joynts of others by peesmeale, and broiling on
ye coles eate ye collops of their flesh in their
sight whilst they live.*" Such a prospect
might well "*move the very bowels of men to
grate within them, and make ye weake to
quake and tremble.*" All honour to the men
and stout-hearted women who braved these
dangers, not altogether imaginary! That
they had much to fear is unquestionable.
The shedding of blood such as that so lightly
mentioned by Capt. Smith, and again by Mr.
Dermer, and further the villainous slave
raiding perpetrated by a miscreant named
Hunt, who had carried off some twenty-four
of the natives intending to sell them as
slaves in Spain (among whom was Squanto,
the future interpreter), had incensed the
Indians against white men. How far the
Colonists might have met with perils such
as they feared we cannot say, but it happened
that the way had been prepared for them.

A terrible sickness, such as the people seemed specially subject to, had desolated the country, leaving at Accomack not a man alive save Squanto, and Bradford describes the traces of this grievous visitation which were seen by an exploring party shortly after their arrival, —the bones of the dead lying still unburied on the ground. Thus they were able to plant themselves firmly until they were strong enough to repel attack.

The land, on their arrival, to Bradford's gaze, at any rate, presented but a dismal prospect. "*What could they see but a hideous and desolate wilderness, full of wild beasts and wild men?*" But it improved on further acquaintance. In the next year a letter written home by one of the company gives a far more encouraging picture: "*Indians round us peaceable and friendly. Country pleasant and temperate, yielding vines, walnuts, chestnuts, small nuts and plums, flowers, roots and herbs; no place hath more gooseberries and strawberries, nor better. There is timber. Turkies, quails, pigeons, partridges, lakes abounding with fish and fowl, otters and beavers. Better grain cannot be than the Indian corn.* And moreover *we are all freeholders, the rent day doth not trouble us."*

These words, which are borne out by other accounts, describe the natural resources of the country, on which they came more and more to rely. It was thought that they would gain their livelihood mainly upon fishing. It was fishing that, in Captain Smith's view, constituted the wealth of the country, an estimate for which the name of the great headland, Cape Cod, might be taken as a justification. And many attempts at fishing were made, but from some cause or other, perhaps because they were landsmen, who had had no experience of seafaring life, the men of Plymouth seem to have made but a poor business of it. "*It was,*" says Governor Bradford, "*a thing fatal to this colony*"; and again, "*they had always lost by fishing."* The staple of their trade was in beaver and otter skins, and clapboard (*i.e.* wood cut into "feather-edged" planks) for the home market. And they soon found another

market among the Indians, with whom they
bartered beads, knives, cloth, and other
home-procured articles.   But it is interesting that they soon began to raise the commodities for their trading in their new home.
It was not very long before they found demand
among the Indians for as much corn as they
could grow ; and another most profitable com-
modity was introduced to them by the Dutch,
viz. Whampampeag, the trade in which produced, Bradford observes, quite an alteration
in the disposition of the Indians towards them,
so greatly did they come to desire it.   This
whampampeag, called sometimes whampam,
sometimes peag, and sometimes by the whole
name, consisted of shells, or rather the middle
part of the clam shell, strung on threads.   Out
of the shell was cut a small cylinder about a
quarter of an inch deep, and being bored and
strung was used amongst some tribes of the
Indians as money.   The strings were also
woven into bracelets, of six threads in a row,
and into girdles of many rows.   It was
reckoned at a later time at the value of 5*s.*

per fathom for white whampam and 10*s*. per
fathom for black or purple.   Bradford tells
us that the Narrigansets and Pequents, keeping it to themselves, prided themselves greatly
upon the possession.   But when a more
general trade was established, the Indians
took to it with great eagerness, and to it he
attributes the enriching not only of the
Colonists, but also, though the reasoning is a
little obscure, of the Indians also.   And it
became a source of not unmixed benefit, for
the Indians became rich, powerful, and proud,
and able to purchase guns, powder and shot,
a development of very ominous character.

The Colonists were for a very long time
dependent for articles of domestic use upon
the home market, and very curiously interesting are the lists of commodities which are
sent, or which their agents are commissioned
to purchase for them.   Coats and cloaks were
in great request in the early days of the Colony,
and it is noted as a circumstance of great
good-fortune that the first ship which came
out brought some "*Burching lane suits*," a

description of articles on which some light is
thrown by Stow in his "*Survey of London*"
(1633). He tells us that Birchin lane (so called
after Birchover the builder) "*hath been inhabited
for the most part by wealthy drapers.*"[1] As
the Colony gets richer, Bastable (*i.e.* Barn-
stable) rugs and metheglin (*i.e.* mead, a drink
made of honey, and fermented) become
articles of import. And there are singularly
detailed lists of goods wanted for private use,
such as linen cloths, bed-ticks, stockings, tape,
pins, rugs, &c.

The intercourse with home was not carried on without much risk and frequent loss,
partly by reason of storms, but also from
enemies and pirates. The first ship carrying
a cargo to England (valued at £500) was
captured by the French, and all the goods
seized. Mr. Cushman, who was made a
prisoner, but afterwards set free, tells us,
indeed, that they were hoping to recover these

[1] His description continues: "*From Birchin Lane on
that side of the street, down to the stocks, had (for the most
part) dwelling there fripperers and upholders that sold old
apparel or household stuffs.*"

losses in France. But whether this actually happened we are not told. Besides risks from greater enemies, such as France and Spain, there were pirates innumerable upon the seas; one ship was captured by pirates off the coast of Ireland: another fell a prey to a Turkish warship almost within sight of Plymouth (in Old England). It is difficult to realise the insecurity of traffic from such enemies in these more secure times. Lawlessness and turbulence were rife outside the pale of settled cities, and until the establishment of the Massachusetts Colonies there were probably not many places on the coast of the bay where men could live at peace, and under the shelter of law, besides Plymouth. Within the town itself, Bradford and his assistants seem to have ruled over a quiet and law-abiding people. Our manuscript, at any rate, contains comparatively few records of crime, and it was not for many years that the Colony required a prison. Still, mention does arise now and again of delinquents being whipped for thieving and other immoralities.

Visitors who so offended were shipped off to other places ; very grievous offences were, however, visited with great severity. And in the midst of much that accords in thought and spirit with our modern ideas it is somewhat startling to come upon the deliberately expressed opinion of a grave divine that, in his judgment, "*in matters of highest consequence magistrates may proceed so far to bodily torments as racks, hote irons,*" &c. to extract a confession. However, New England was probably not behind the rest of the world in the seventeenth century.

It is pleasant to note that on one occasion, when the question was raised whether a criminal intention should be visited with the same punishment as the effected crime, Bradford's opinion inclined to the more merciful view. He doubts, too, whether adultery is a capital offence.

But we must bring to a conclusion this sketch of the land and of the times in which our narrative is placed. And we cannot do better than conclude with a description of

H

a natural feature which has, alas! only too often given a lamentable interest to the history of America, viz. its liability to hurricanes. The following is a description of one which took place in the year 1635 :

This year, y 14 *or* 15 *of August* (*being Saturday,*) *was such a mighty storme of wind, and raine, as none living in these parts, either English, or Indeans ever saw. Being like* (*for y* time it continued*), *to those Hauricanes, and tuffons that writers make mention of in y* Indeas* ; *it began in y* morning, a litle before day, and grue not by degrees, but came with violence in y* begining, to y* great amasmente of many. It blew downe sundry houses, and uncovered others* ; *diverse vessells were lost at sea, and many more in extreme danger* ; *It caused y* sea to swell* (*to y* southward of this place*) *about* 20 *foote right up and downe* ; *and made many of the Indeans to clime into trees for their saftie* ; *it tooke of y* borded roofe of a house which belonged to this plantation at Manamet, and floted it to*

another place, the posts still standing in y
ground. And if it had continued long
without y shifting of ye wind, it is like it*
would have drouned some parte of y cuntrie.*
It blew downe many hundered thousands of
trees, turning up the stronger by the roots,
and breaking the hiegher pine trees of, in the
midle; and y tall yonge oaks, & walnut*
trees of good biggnes were wound like a withe,
very strang, and fearfull to behould. It
begane in y south'st, and parted toward y*
south east, and vered sundry ways, but y
greatest force of it here was from y former*
quarters; it continued not (in y extremitie)*
above 5 or 6 houers, but y violence begane to*
abate. The signes, and marks of it will re-
maine this 100 years in these parts wher it
was sorest. The moone suffered a great eclips
the 2 night after it.

IV

WILLIAM BRADFORD, AS AUTHOR, MAN, AND STATESMAN

In the " History of Plymouth Plantation " we have William Bradford presented to us in the aspect of author, autobiographer, and historian. Of course the History is the chief, indeed the only consciously undertaken object of his writing.   And as a history, from the importance of the events he chronicles and from his unique relation to them, as well as from its own intrinsic merit, his work is beyond price.   But a history of events so essentially connected with his name and influence, of which it was so true, though he would never have said it, *quorum pars magna fui*, becomes an involuntary autobiography. It was not his desire to pose before the world.   On the contrary, he keeps himself severely in the background, and hardly ever permits himself to appear in the story except under the impersonal designation of the "Governor." Hardly an allusion personal to himself occurs, except in some annotations made later in life. But this reticence both in what he tells us, and in what he keeps to himself, is strongly characteristic, and adds another expressive, though unconscious, touch to the autobiographical portrait. As an author, his conception and treatment of his subject, his style, language, and, not least, handwriting itself, have all a high degree of literary interest as specimens of the English of the time, and of the culture attained by a man of the people. But there is an interest deeper still in tracing the character of the man in the style of the author, even as the man himself is formed by the history which he relates.

Governor Bradford's manuscript is a large quarto of some 280 pages, written for the most part on one side of the paper only, though in some parts the History covers both sides ;

and some of the blank pages are used for additional notes written by Bradford himself at a later period, and for a few subsequent annotations by Mr. Thomas Prince, who used the work for his " *New England Chronology.*" There are a few straggling entries of facts, relating to the later history of the book, written on the outer leaves. The first few pages are used by Bradford as a note-book for his Hebrew Studies. The History occupies 270 pages, and is followed by an Appendix giving a record of the persons who came over in the first ship, written in 1650. Against Bradford's own name someone has written "*who dyed 9th of May* 1658," and has also added a few notes as to survivors of the first party as late as 1698. The volume is bound in white vellum like an account-book, and is somewhat discoloured.

The History itself is written in handwriting of singular clearness (the letters all formed separately), suggestive of unwearied patience and conscientiousness. In some places it is minute and close, with 59 lines of, on an average, 16 words to the line, in a column of 10 × 7 in., every letter formed with a distinctness as perfect as that of printing. On other pages the writing is larger and less regular. The work falls into two divisions. The first part consists of an introductory chapter, leading to the story of the flight to Leyden and of the subsequent history of the Pilgrims, up to the point of their discovery and occupation of New Plymouth. With their establishment in their new home the writer begins his second book, prefacing it with these words :

The rest of this history (If God give me life, and opportunitie) I shall for brevitie sake, handle by way of annalls, noteing only the heads of principall things and passages as they fell in order of time ; and may seeme to be profitable to know, or to make use of. And this may be as ye 2 booke.

But, though the history is thenceforward recorded "*by way of annalls*," there is evidence to show that it was actually written in its present form at a later period and all together.

As Mr. Doyle has lately pointed out,[1] the
state of preservation and cleanness of the
paper are incompatible with a course of entries
continued during a period of thirty years.
The author, moreover, himself states that
"*these scribbled writings*" were begun
"*about y*ᵉ *year* 1630, *and so peeced up at
times of leasure afterwards.*" But these
"*scribbled writings*" seem to have been only
the notes from which the History was afterwards compiled. As early as the fifty-seventh
page, in the record of the year 1620, we
are informed that the peace with Massasoyt
"*hath now continued this twenty-four years,*"
which brings us at least to the year 1644 as the
time of writing. Some additional notes on the
blank pages are dated 1646. The last entry
relates to the year 1646, and records that Mr.
Winslow went to England in that year, and
"*hath now bene absente this* 4 *years,*" *i.e.*
until 1650. The heading for the years 1647
and 1648 is written, though no record follows.

[1] In his introduction to the facsimile reprint of the MS.
lately published.

The Appendix is distinctly dated 1650. We are justified, therefore, in regarding the history as the work of Bradford's later years, written in the maturity of his judgment, and in view of the issue to which the events were tending.

The English in which it is written is that of the English Bible, or perhaps we should rather say the more popular language of the "*Pilgrim's Progress.*" It is a language which Bradford uses with great effect. His style is a little stiff, perhaps, to our notions, and now and then somewhat involved. But usually it flows with transparent clearness. He chooses his words with great felicity, and seems to have them equally at his command, whether wielding them with terrible emphasis like the blows of a hammer in indignant denunciation, or pouring them out in lucid narrative or in the eloquent expression of deep and tender pathos. The vigour, the terseness, the expressiveness of his style are well illustrated in the extracts which have been given in the pages of this book. The spelling is

throughout irregular, though not illiterate, and
here and there we come upon expressions and
constructions which have become archaic.[1]
Scriptural allusions abound ; and the style is
frequently enlivened by homely phrases and
illustrations, colloquial in character, but admi-
rably adapted to express the writer's meaning.
For instance, Robinson brought his Ar-
minian opponent to an *apparent* (*i.e.* evident)
nonpluss.   Blackwell betrayed one of his
friends "*that so he might slip his own neck
out of ye coler.*" "*He wone ye bp's favour (but
lost ye Lord's),*" (p. 25). Oldham had been
a "*chief stickler*" in a former faction, and
"*ramped more like a furious beast than a
man,*" until "*he was clapt up a while.*" Lyford, who opened other men's letters, is "*this
slye marchante,*" *i.e.* fellow, and of these two
the following illustration seems to have been
used in the public court: "*like the Hedg-
hogg whom ye conny in a stormy day (in
pittie) receaved into her borrow, would not
be content to take part with her, but in the*

[1] See note on page 130.

end with her sharp pricks forst ye poore conny to forsake her owne borrow, so these two," &c. There is telling sarcasm in the following : "*for shuch men (hypocritical ministers) pretend much for poor souls, but they will looke to their wages and conditions, if that be not to their content, let poor souls doe what they will they will shift for themselves, and seeke poore souls somewher els, among richer bodys*" (p. 128). Of the same character is the description of the man "*who was so drunke y^t he rane his owne nose upon ye pointe of a sword y^t one held before him*"; and the typical Englishman speaks in the account of the French surprise of Penobscot : "*and many French complements they used, and congees they made*" till they had cajoled the occupants out of their arms. P. 188 (a).

Illustrations like these might be multiplied indefinitely. We must pass on from the consideration of the style to gather some of the indications given us in the book of the personal history of the man and his character.

It has been mentioned that he tells us very little about his own doings, except so far as they are connected with the general fortunes of the Colony. He seems to have joined the congregation at Scrooby at its commencement, and he writes of the persecutions they endured as one who had felt them. He was then about seventeen years old. From his vivid description of the flight from England —telling how for instance the Dutch captain swore his country's oath, "*Sacramente*" and weighed anchor—and of the storm which followed, the water running into their mouths and ears, as the ship seemed "*foundered in ye sea*," the ejaculations of the mariners and of the passengers, and how "*if modestie would suffer*" he could tell of their prayers—we infer that he was one of the first party that thus escaped. Of his own life at Leyden he makes no mention, and all that we can gather of his position among the refugees is conveyed by the fact that his initials with those of two others occur at the end of a letter written in the name of the

whole body.   When the party reached
America, he tells us that he was among those
who were stricken with the disease, and was
much beholden to Brewster and Standish
for their kind offices.   To the mention of a
specially brutal answer given by a sailor to one
in his sickness who desired but a small can of
beer a little note is added in the margin—
"*which was this author himself.*"   He tells us
that on the death of Carver " *William Bradford was chosen governor in his stead—being
not yet recovered of his ilnes in which he had
been near ye point of death.*"   From this
point until the resignation of his Patent in
1640 we read of him only as "*the governor.*"
The facts that he left a young son behind
when he sailed from England, that his wife
died soon after their arrival, that he married
again and had four children, we learn but
from the Appendix.   This reticence seems
significant not only of his modest and reserved
character, but also of his absorption in the
fortunes of the Church and Colony to which
he devoted his whole self and work.   No

man had a higher ideal of public spirit and
of the subordination of private to public
interest than he. He quotes with approval
of his beloved master, Mr. Robinson, that
"*none did more offend him than those that were
close, and cleaving to themselves.*"   One main
source of the success with which the weak
and struggling Colony came through the
overwhelming difficulties and hardships of the
early years was the public spirit and cohesion
of its members, tried, as they were, at more
than one critical period in their history, and
of this public spirit none partook more fully,
or set a more noble example than the
Governor.   Indeed, it may be thought that
Bradford carries this absorption in the affairs
of Plymouth even to the fault of a certain
narrowing of his sympathies. He is all for
Plymouth ; and his interest in the affairs of
his neighbours, in the rise and progress of
other Colonies as they grew up around him,
even in the great migrations of his co-
religionists to Boston Bay in 1630, is but
incidental, so far only as they affected his

own beloved community. But if his affections
were somewhat narrowed, making him, as we
may imagine, a man of but few intimate
friends, they were very deep and break out
at times from his habitual reserve with strong
and pathetic emotion. Witness the tender
and touching account of the departure from
Leyden, and the sorrowful leave-takings of
parting friends. Witness, too, his devoted
affection for his friends Robinson and Brewster. To others, as to Cushman, he can give
a just and generous appreciation ; to these
he gives his heart. And his strong yearning
for love and confidence, often characteristic
of a reserved nature, and his longing for it
both in public and private relations, when it
seemed to be lost, is expressed with passionate
intensity in a note written in old age con-
trasting the latter with the former state of
the Colony :

*O sacred bond, whilst inviollably pre-
served! how sweete and precious were the
fruits, that flowed from ye same! But when*

*this fidelity decayed; then their ruine ap-
proached. O that these anciente members had
not dyed, or been dissipated, if it had been the
will of God, or els that this holy care, and
constante faithfullness had still lived, and
remained with those that survived and were
in times afterwards added unto them. But
(alas) that subtill serpente hath slylie wound
in himselfe, under faire pretences of necessitie,
and ye like, to untwiste those sacred bonds,
and tyes, and as it were insensibly by degrees
to dissolve (or in a great measure) to weaken
ye same. I have been happy, in my first
times, to see, and with much comforte to
injoye, the blessed fruits of this sweete com-
munion, but it is now a parte of my miserie,
in old age to find, and feele ye decay, and wante
therof (in a great measure) and with greefe,
and sorrow of hart to lamente, & bewaile
ye same. And for others warning, and
admonition, (and my own humiliation) doe I
hear note ye same.*

Bradford's deep affection for his "*pore*

people," this poor persecuted Church, and
their confidence in him shown by his
repeated election [1] as Governor, had its roots
in the Puritanism which bound them together in devotion to a common cause.
Puritanism was to them the very Cause of
God, and they were God's people, pledged
by a sacred covenant to stand firm, and to
stand together. And the bond of common
allegiance to their cause had been drawn
closer and stronger by years of fellowship in
persecution, in their perilous venture, in
battling with the difficulties of their situation.
In their principles and aspirations he and
they were in full accord. Bradford was a
Puritan in his devotion to the principles of
Independency, and in the bitter hatred, which
they then involved, of Episcopacy with its
"*courts cannons and ceremonies.*" He was a
Puritan in his ideal of the State exercising
the functions of the Church, and enforcing
by strict discipline, moral and spiritual, its

[1] Twelve times successively, 1621–1632, and eight times
between 1633 and 1646.

I

austere standard of life.   He partook fully
of the strong "*esprit de corps*" which ani-
mated the party, and was very jealous for its
liberty, its purity, and its consistency.   But
he was a man whose personal character preserved him from much of the narrowness
which Calvinism tended to develop.   His
was a Puritanism of the earlier type, which
had not begun to frown upon innocent
culture, in which austerity had not turned to
sourness, nor lost its sympathy with the
many-sided interests of human life.

He is very bitter against the Church of
England, and ruthless in his exultation over
the downfall of Episcopacy.   A note written
in 1646, on the page opposite to that on
which, early in his work, he has recorded
the oppression suffered by the Noncon
formists, gives utterance to an almost savage
triumph.   But his denunciations, though
violent, never degenerate into scurrilous
abuse, such as too often disgraced the contro-
versies of the time.   His religion is practical
rather than doctrinal.   And as he wins our

respect by his own unfeigned piety and uprightness, so he too judges of men by their actual conduct and not by the party they belong to. And he judges individuals with discrimination and often with generosity. He makes no capital out of the fact that Lyford was a clergyman of the Church of England. And even of Oldham he is inclined on one occasion to believe that he was actuated, not by hypocrisy, but by "*some sudden pang of conviction.*"

A devout mind such as his naturally tends to see the hand of Providence in everything, and Bradford has given us a very beautiful description of an occasion on which prayer was answered "*to their owne and ye Indeans admiration.*" There had been a great drought which continued for two months with great heat, "*insomuch yᵉ corne began to wither away, though it was set with fishe the moysture whereof helped it much: yet at length it began to languish sore—upon which they set aparte a solemne day of Humiliation to seek yᵉ Lord by humble and fervente prayer in this great dis-*

trese," and, on that same day, hot and cloud-
less at the beginning, yet "*toward evening it
began to overcast, and shortly after to raine
with shuch sweete and gentle showers, as gave
them cause of rejoyceing and blessing God.*"
But this devout instinct of faith is liable to
perversion in the cause of religious partisan-
ship.   Bradford was not free from the disposition, then only too common, to attribute
the misfortunes of those whom he disliked to
the judgment of God.   There is the story,
for instance, of the "*proud and very profane
young man,*" who, after insulting over the
poor sea-sick passengers, was himself the first
to be stricken with disease and die, from which
our author does not fail to draw the edifying
moral.   But his reverence was too deep and
sincere to allow this dangerous tendency to
carry him away unchecked.   "*God's judgments are unscerchable,*" he says on one occasion, "*neither dare I be bould therwith, but,
however, it shows us y⁵ uncertainty of all
humane things, and what little cause there is
of joying in them, or trusting to them*"

(p. 138). And again, when the Massachusetts people, who had thrust themselves unscrupulously into Connecticut, met with misfortunes there, he remarks, "*which some imputed as a correction from God for their intrution (to ye wrong of others) into y^t place; but I dare not be bould with God's judgments in this kind.*"

Bradford was a man of considerable reading. His familiarity with the Bible (in the Genevan Version) is manifest in the frequent use of Scriptural language, and in the application of illustrations borrowed from the Bible history, such as Gideon's army, the men of Eshcol, Naomi and Orpah, Saul's asses, Ishmael and Gedaliah, &c., used with much quaint originality. But he also shows familiarity with many other books, ancient and contemporary. His reading supplies quotations (taking them in the order in which they occur) from Socrates (the Church historian), Foxe, Eusebius, a famous writer of Dutch commentaries (Emmanuel van Meteren), the "*Goulden Book*" of Marcus Aurelius, Plutarch's "*Life of Cato*," Seneca, Peter Martyr, Purchas, Pliny.   He is familiar with the story of Moses given by a Heathen writer (Tacitus), and with the history of the Taborites and Zisca. And it is evident that he had not only read, but had digested, and could apply with appositeness, the information he had gained.   He was also a careful observer of Nature.   He does not show much appreciation of natural beauty. On the wonders of land and sea and sky he makes no comment.   His first impressions of America reflect only the depression of his own feelings.   He is more ready to recognise the awful majesty of Divine Power in natural phenomena than joy and beauty.   But he has given us descriptions of a hurricane, and of an earthquake, drawn with a careful accuracy of detail and circumstance worthy of modern science.   And there is an account of a visitation of flies in 1633, followed by a pestilence among the Indians, which has a characteristic interest.

*This disease allso swept away many of y*ᵉ

*Indeans from all ye places near adjoyning ;
and ye spring before, espetially all ye month of
May, ther was shuch a quantitie of a great
sorte of flies, like (for bignes) to wasps, or
bumble-bees, which came out of holes in y^e
ground, and replenished all ye woods, and eate
ye green things ; and made shuch a constante
yelling noyes, as made all ye woods ring of
them, and ready to deafe ye hearers ; they
have not by ye English been heard, or seen
before or since. But ye Indeans tould them
y^t sicknes would follow, and so it did in June,
July, August, and ye cheefe heat of sommer.*

One further trait of character must be no-
ticed, without which our sketch of Governor
Bradford would be incomplete, viz. his
possession of the invaluable gift of humour.
It is a gift which few leaders of men have
been without, and which has oftentimes
added much to the influence of its pos-
sessors.   A sense of the ridiculous in themselves or in others has been to many men, or
might have been, a wholesome corrective

of exaggeration and intolerance. It is
good that the stern features of authority,
especially of Puritan austerity, should sometimes relax into a smile. Humour is invaluable to a statesman, and Bradford was
fortunate in his possession of the gift. It is
shown in many of his comments and illustrations, as for instance in his allusion to the
Romans who forsook Cato in Utica praying
to be excused "*though they could not all be
Catos,*" and in his quotation of Seneca,
"*That a great part of libertie is a well
governed belly.*" His description of Lyford's
false humility, which "*indeed made them
ashamed, he so bowed and cringed unto them,*"
shows the same characteristic, not only in his
shrewd insight into the character of the man,
but also in his lively telling of the story. There
is, moreover, a grim humour in the punishment which Oldham was condemned to suffer
—made to run the gauntlet between two files
of soldiers, each of whom gave him a thump
behind with the butt-end of his musket as

he passed, and so sent him off to mend his manners.

Nor is it only in his narrative and in his shrewd perceptions that Bradford's humour is shown. The same gift helped him to deal successfully with practical difficulties, where a heavier hand and harsher manner might have provoked worse troubles. An instance of such dealing is given us, with considerable enjoyment by himself, in the account of the newcomers in 1621 who declined to go to their duties on Christmas Day, saying it was against their conscience to work on that day. "*So ye gov^r tould them that, if they made it a matter of conscience, he would spare them, till they were better informed.*" But when, on returning from work, he found them in the street at play, "*he tooke away their implements, and tould them that was against his conscience that they should play & others worke ; if they made ye keeping of it a matter of devotion, let them kepe their houses.*"

Of Bradford's general administration of

its affairs, the Colony of Plymouth itself is his lasting monument. Called to undertake the government almost single-handed at the early age of thirty, he brought the community through all the perils and difficulties of its troubled infancy by the force of his own upright character, his strong common-sense, his courage, wisdom, and faith. He could act boldly and promptly in the time of danger, as for instance when he returned the defiant message of the Narrigansets with like defiance. It wanted no small courage for a little body of some 90 people to challenge a tribe that could put 900 or 1,000 warriors into the field. In vigorous action he was never wanting.

The scheme by which the Colony became the purchasers of the property of the Adventurers was a bold stroke of policy. But bolder still was the action of the "*undertakers*," of whom we cannot doubt that Bradford was the inspiring genius, by which they hired the trade for six years, undertaking its debts. It was taking upon

their individual shoulders the responsibilities
of the whole body. It was risking personal
ruin to save the community. And it be
tokened a brave confidence in the latent
resources of the Colony, of which it proved
itself not unworthy. Bradford's strength lay
in seizing the bearings of the situation and in
meeting them with promptness and vigour.

He saw at once the danger that was
looming behind the factious conduct of Lyford
and Oldham, danger of an irreparable schism.
And he was prompt, vigorous and circumspect
in his action. In the night when the ship
which carried home the letters of the con-
spirators put to sea, he followed in a small
boat and took copies of such as proved to be
what he expected. Possessed of proof, he
watched his opportunity, waited till the
mischief had come to a head, and then
struck home, with irresistible effect. And
the hand which was prompt to strike was
not wanting, when the occasion offered, to
heal. When the break-up of the company
caused the transfer of its property to the

Colony, the opportunity arose for closing the schism between the *"generals"* and the *"particulars,"* which was ever threatening to rend the State in two. There was some wavering of opinion as to how the newly organised community was to bear itself towards the *"untowarde persons"* who were in the midst of it. But *"the gov^r and counsell with other of their cheef friends"* wisely seeing that *"for ye present, excepte peace and union were preserved, they should be able to doe nothing but indanger to over-throw all, now that other tyes and bonds were taken away, therefore they resolved to take in all amongst them."* And so the Colony was restored again to that unity of interest and sentiment which was necessary for its very existence.

Governor Bradford has been described by Mr. Doyle in eloquent words as the prototype of the long beadroll of American Presidents who have borne rule by the free choice of their brethren. From Bradford onward "America has never wanted men who with no early training in political life, and lacking much that the Old World has deemed needful in her rulers, have yet by inborn strength of mind, and lofty public spirit, shown themselves in all things worthy of high office." And the testimony is well deserved. For the requirements of her early existence, Plymouth had in him the very man she needed. Brave, indefatigable, public spirited, keen sighted, uniting an ardent jealousy for her welfare with an entire abnegation of self, he elevated the whole tone of life, public and private, by the example of his blameless and sincerely religious life. He was the ideal governor to watch over her struggling infancy, to direct the simple administration of her almost patriarchal government, and to regulate the rapidly growing forces of her vigorous youth. For the difficult task of ruling strong-willed men by their own consent, without the aid of traditional authority, as in old established States, his qualification lay in the influence of his personal character. And for the immediate needs of present policy his

statesmanship was sufficient. He could
watch for fresh openings for trade, and
establish outposts in well-chosen positions.
He could foresee that Plymouth must grow,
and that it was needful, in laying out the
allotments of land, to provide not only for
concentration as a means of strength, but also
for extension by the influx of new comers.
But that his statesmanship should rise to the
capacity of genius, and conceive a policy for
the more distant future of Plymouth, and its
expansion beyond the limits of a single town
and a local congregation, was perhaps hardly
to be expected. As a matter of fact, the
instincts and necessities of the people were
driving them on to wider aims than Bradford
could understand or approve. He more than
once complains of the consequences of growing wealth—that it was tending to dispersion
of the Colony, which would be its ruin. From
one point of view, his direction of the policy
of the State was a series of concessions.
It is, indeed, no small tribute to his wisdom that he knew how to make concessions

with a good grace. But they show a limited view.

An instance arose in the case of Duxbury, a growing offshoot of the mother-Colony, which was attracting to itself some of the wealthier Colonists, and claimed some amount of local independence and a separate church. The prospect filled Bradford with apprehension, and was only accepted with reluctance, accompanied by expedients calculated to stem the rising and dangerous tide. But it was in vain. The process of expansion went on. It was the destiny of Plymouth to grow, a destiny which she could only renounce at peril of her life. That Bradford failed to comprehend this, that it inspired him only with a lament over his beloved Plymouth left "*like an anciente mother growne olde and forsaken of her children*," shows that in its ultimate aims his statesmanship was at fault, and he had mistaken his ideal. It was like the solicitude of a loving but over-anxious father, fearing to entrust his children with that future for which his parental faithfulness had indeed been preparing them.

Bradford's history takes us to the year 1646. At its conclusion he had still some years to live. He describes himself as now grown old, though he had not yet attained the allotted term of years. But it may well be that he was grown old in labours. Of the quiet retirement of these later days a touching memorial remains in those notes of Hebrew study which, as has been said, occupy the first pages of his manuscript. The notes are prefaced by these affecting words :

Though I am growne aged, yet I have had a longing desire, to see with my owne eyes, something of that most ancient language, and holy tongue, in which the Law and oracles of God were write ; and in which God, and angels spake to the holy patriarks of old time ; and what names were given to things, from the creation. And though I canote attaine to much herein, yet I am re-freshed, to have seen some glimpse hereof (as Moyses saw the land of Canan afarr of) ; my *aime and desire is, to see how the words and phrases lye in the holy texte; and to discerne somewhat of the same, for my own contente.*

No more touching conclusion could be given to his strenuous toilsome life than this peaceful picture of the old man solacing his declining days with the contemplation, like Moses from the top of Pisgah, of Divine hopes and eternal promises, which endear to him even the very letters in which they were written. Of him it may truly be said that he was

One who never turned his back but marched breast forward,
    Never doubted clouds would break,
Never dreamed, though right were worsted, wrong would triumph,
Held we fall to rise, are baffled to fight better,
    Sleep to wake.

K

NOTES ON SOME OF THE CURIOUS WORDS AND FORMS OF EXPRESSION OCCURRING IN THE MS.

THE following are some, though not a complete list, of the curious words and expressions which are met with in the MS.

"Tragedies which he (Satan) *put in ure*," p. 2, *i.e.*, put in operation ; connected with French œuvre.

Chatchpoule officers, p. 8, the Mediæval Latin is chassipullus, " fowl-catcher " ; Murray's Dict. quotes Wicliffe's Bible, i. Sam. xix. 20, " Saule sent catchpollis to take David." The word seems equivalent to " officers." But there is an illustration of a catchpole, an implement, on p. 1021 of Green's *Short History*, vol. 3, Illust. Edit.

Murderers, p. 58, a name for small guns which were fixed on the decks of ships to sweep them clear of boarding parties. Captain John Smith enumerates *murderers* in his list of " Ordinance and peeces" required for a ship of war ; see *Accidence for Young Seamen*, Arber's reprint, p. 799.

Snaphance ordnance, p. 265, a technical term of gunnery (called also Snapphahn or Asnaphan) meaning a small hand gun or pistol fired with a flint lock as distinguished from a matchlock.

Speaking of guns, Bradford, p. 158, says that
the very sight of a gun (though *out of kilter*) was
originally a terror to the Indians. The phrase
out of kilter is of doubtful origin, and used only
colloquially in this form ; it means *out of order.*
Barrow speaks of organs (musical instruments) *out
of kelter.*

" He that *cund* the ship," p. 99, *i.e.*, conned, that
is, kept a look-out. The word still survives as a
nautical term in " conning tower." Other nautical
terms are found on p. 46 : " the seas were so high
they could not bear a *knote* of sail, but were
forced to *hull,* and as they *lay at hull* a young man
by a *seele* (*i.e.*, sudden roll or heel) was thrown over-
board." Again, on p. 208 it is complained that the
captain " did not *lay his ship better to pass* " : the
word *to pass* is perhaps connected with the phrase
take *a pass* round a block. Or it may simply mean
" better *for effect.*" In another place it is said that
a ship was so overladen and stuffed between decks
that " she was *walte* and could not bear sail."

In one of Mr. Robinson's letters, p. 115, he
writes " what *a hanck* these men have over the
professors you know." The word *hank* means a
skein or coil of yarn ; to have a *hank* over others is
to have them entangled.

Eftsone, p. 132, is to us an unfamiliar word ;
eft means again : *eftsoon*, soon again.

Junkats, p. 159, sweetmeats so-called because it is said they were served on rushes (juncus).

Extravagants, p. 128, is used in its etymological meaning, *i.e.*, wanderers away from their own proper place.

There is a curious phrase (p. 174) in the account of the disagreements between the partners at Plymouth and at London. Mr. Winslow is despatched to England "to see how *the squars* wente." The word *square* seems sometimes to have been used in the sense of *quarrel*, and so it may be here. Another quaint and expressive phrase occurs in connection with these disagreements : "Mr. Allerton doth in a sort wholly now desert them (the partners), and having *brought them into the briers*, he leaves them to get out as they can." In further correspondence on the same matter we find the expression *to shadow it the more*, apparently in the sense of making more explicit, as of completing an outline by filling in the shadows. And again, p. 227, the Plymouth people complain that they are charged with so much of that which they never had *nor drunk for*, where "drinking" seems to be used as an equivalent for the bargain, of which it was a concomitant.

Another unfamiliar use of the word drink is found in the next page, where some men, designing murder, invite an Indian to *drink tobacco*. To drink, meaning to inhale, tobacco was then a common expression.

We find the word *rendezvous* (spelled in various ways) in common use, and the terms *adventurer*, *undertaker*, have a well understood meaning in connection with commercial transactions. *Condescend unto* occurs frequently in the sense of *agree to*. *Baffoyling*, p. 119, is a curious spelling for baffling, and may have an etymological origin.

Some curious Christian names occur in the list of passengers by the *Mayflower*. One *Desire* Minter was maidservant to Mr. Carver. Mr. Brewster had two sons, *Love* and *Wrasling*. Allerton's three children were called Bartholomew, *Remember* and Mary. A child born at sea was appropriately called *Oceanus*, an elder sister was called *Damaris*. And the child of William White and Susanna his wife, born on shipboard, after their arrival received the name *Peregrine* ; his elder brother was *Resolved*. This *Resolved* was still living in 1690.

A CHRONOLOGICAL SUMMARY OF GOVERNOR BRADFORD'S NARRATIVE

Events in History of Plymouth	*Contemporary Events* [1]
1590. *Birth of Wm. Bradford*	
1602. Capt. Gosnold explores Cape Cod, 46	1603. *Accession of James I.*
	1604. *Hampton Court Conference*
1606-7. Formation of congregation at *Scrooby*, under Mr. Clifton; Mr. Robinson, Mr. Brewster, and *Wm. Bradford (aged 17)* being members, 6	1606-7. Colony established at Virginia *Plymouth or North Virginia Company formed*
1607. First attempt to leave England	
1608. (Spring.) Escape from England. Most of the men were hurried off first by themselves; after stormy passage of fourteen days, being carried to coast of Norway, they arrive in Holland, 9 The rest of the men and the women and children follow at intervals. Settle at Amsterdam, and remain about a year, 24	1608. *Formation of Protestant Union and Catholic League in Germany*
	1609-21. *Twelve years' truce between Dutch and Spaniards*
1610. Remove to Leyden	1610. *May 14. Assassination of Henry IV. of France*
	1612. *First English factory established at Surat*
	1614. Capt. John Smith explores coast of New England

[1] Some other contemporary events are noted in italics by way of illustration, besides those mentioned in the Narrative. The figures given refer to the pages in the Bradford MS.

Events in History of Plymouth	*Contemporary Events*
1617. Two representatives sent to England to negotiate with Virginia Company and with Privy Council for freedom of religion, 18 They return, 19	**1617.** Frenchmen cast ashore at Cape Cod abused by Indians, 60
— Nov. Two other messengers, John Carver and Robert Cushman, sent to England	
— Dec. 15. Articles of Inducement signed at Leyden, 21	
1618. Jan. 27. "Declarations" in an- (1617 swer to questions of Privy O.S.) Council, 22	**1618.** *Outbreak of Thirty Years' War in Germany* *Kepler at Linz* Mr. Blackwell's disastrous expedition to Virginia, 24
— (?) Oct. Patent granted by Virginia Company, 26	— *Oct. 29. Execution of Sir Walter Raleigh* — *Nov. 13. Synod of Dort*
1618–19. Mr. Weston comes to Leyden and persuades Colonists to make terms with him and fellow-adventurers and seek patent from New England Company, 27	**1618–19.** *Revival of North Virginia Company as New England Company* Dermer captured by Indians, 59
1620. June 1. Agreement drawn up by adventurers, 28	**1620.** June 30. Dermer's letter about Plymouth, 58 Death of Dermer, 60
— June 10. Colonists protest against terms of agreement, 31	
— July 22. First emigrants sail from Delfshaven, 36. Arrive at Southampton	
— July 27. Mr. Robinson's letter from Leyden.	
— Aug. 5. *Mayflower* and *Speedwell* start from Southampton, 42 Put in at Dartmouth, 42	
— Aug. 17. Cushman's letter from Dartmouth, 43	
— Sail again : 100 leagues without Land's End find they must return again. Put in at Plymouth, 42	

Events in History of Plymouth	*Contemporary Events*
1620. Sept. 6. Smaller ship being left behind, the larger with 102 passengers puts to sea again	
— Nov. 9 (about). Reach the land	
— Nov. 11. Ship anchored in Cape Cod Harbour, 46	
— Nov. 15. First exploring expedition (*Pamet River*) find corn, 49	1620. Nov. About this time Mrs. Susanna White delivered of son, Peregrine, the first English child born in New England
Second expedition in Shallop explore the same bay; bring away corn, 49	— *Nov. New patent granted to New England Company* .
— Dec. 6. Third expedition sail to bottom of the bay (*Namskaket*), 50	
— Dec. 8. "First encounter," 51	
— Dec. 9. Enter Plymouth Harbour, 51	
— Dec. 10. Sunday. Rest	
— Dec. 11. Return to the ship, 53 Covenant of Union signed, 54	
— Dec. 16. Ship anchored in Plymouth Harbour, 53	
— Dec. 25. First house begun John Carver, governor, 54	
1621. Jan. 14. Fire at house of (1620 rendezvous, 61 O.S.)	
— Jan. Visitation of sickness, 54	
— Feb. Fifty of company die: only six or seven untouched by disease, 55	
— March 16. Samoset (English-speaking Indian) visits the settlement, 56	
Comes again with Squanto Visit of Massasoyt (Sachem of *Pocanawkits*). Peace concluded with the Indians, which lasted twenty-four years, 57	
Begin to plant corn, 61	
Ship (*Mayflower*) sent back England, 61	

Events in History of Plymouth	Contemporary Events
1621. April. Death of Carver, 62 Wm. Bradford[1] elected Governor, with Isaac Allerton as assistant, 62	
— May 12. The first marriage, 62	
— July 2. Ed. Winslow and Hopkins, sent to visit Massasoyt at Sowams, see remains of Indians who perished in plague three years before, 63	
— End of July. John Billington loses himself in wood : is recovered at Nawset. Repayment made to Indians for corn taken in previous November, 63 Arrival of Hobamack Hobamack and Squanto threatened by Indians	
— Aug. 14. Expedition sent to recover Squanto, 64	
— Sept. 18. Shallop, with 10 men, sent to explore Massachusetts, 64 Harvest being gathered, a short term of prosperity ensues	
— Nov. 9. Arrival of the *Fortune* with Cushman and 35 others, 65 Letter from Weston Patent obtained, 66, 67 Agreement with adventurers signed, 67	
— Nov. 23. *Fortune* sent back with 500*l.* of skins, &c., 67–69 Captured by French Narrigansets send defiant message. The Governor's answer Colony put on half-allowance of food, 69 Settlement surrounded with pale, and defence organised	
— Dec. 25. Play in the streets stopped	
1622. Second expedition to Massachusetts Alarm about Narrigansets, 71	**1622.** *March* 22. *Massacre of* 347 *colonists by Indians at Virginia*

[1] From this point onwards, when no other Governor is mentioned, is to be understood that Bradford held that office.

Events in History of Plymouth	Contemporary Events
1622. May. A boat arrives from a ship of Weston's (the *Sparrow*) in Damarin's Cove, 72	
Letter intimating resolution of several adventurers to separate from the Company, 74	
Fort and meeting-house built, 90	
Arrival of the *Charity* and *Swan*, a pinnace, 75	
Bringing letters ominous of coming change from adventurers, and 60 men, 78	
Weston's men in Massachusetts, 92	
News of calamity in Virginia, 79	
In stress of famine (rations at ¼ lb. of bread per day) thefts of corn occur; the thieves "well whipt," 90 [1]	
— Sept. Expedition to try to explore south of cape. Death of Squanto, 92	
1623. Weston's people in Massachusetts in great straits and danger from Indians. Massasoit, being sick and relieved by friends from Plymouth, reveals a conspiracy to cut off Weston's people. Captain Standish goes with relief party and rescues Weston's men, who abandon their colony, 94, 95	
Weston himself arrives. Governor assigns temporary allotments of land to individuals. Failure of communism, 95, 96	
— June. Arrival of Capt. Francis West, Admiral of New England, 100	
— July. Arrival of the *Anne* (44 tons) with 50 people, many of whom have to be sent back again, 100	
And several "Particulars" who are allowed to settle, 103	
— Sept. Arrival of Capt. Robt.	

The pagination of the manuscript here leaps from 79 to 90.

Events in History of Plymouth	*Contemporary Events*
Gorges, General Governor of New England, to assume government of colony, 104	
1623. Sept. Calls Weston to account Settles in Massachusetts, 105	
Fire in colony	
Attempted extension of trade southward : a pinnace sent to Narrigansets to take up corn and beaver; cannot compete with the Dutch. Pinnace, on return, wrecked on Brown's Island, 108	1623. " Scattering beginnings " at Pascataway and Monahigen, 107
1624. Bradford governor with five assistants, 108	1624. *Cardinal Richelieu minister in France*
Pinnace sunk near Damarin's Cove, 109	
Some of the Company join the " Particulars," 109	
Arrival of Winslow, bringing three heifers and a bull (the first cattle brought to the colony), 109	
Letters from Mr. Sherley, &c., 110	
Objections made against the colony (answers thereto), 112	
Letters from Mr. Robinson at Leyden, 113	
A patent for Cape Anne	
Three " eminent persons," viz. a ship's carpenter, a saltmaker, and a preacher	
Beginning of permanent allotments of land, 116	
Death of ship's carpenter, 116	
Failure of saltmaker, 117	
The minister, Lyford, begins to plot with Oldham, 118	
Suspicions being roused, the Governor intercepts Lyford's and Oldham's letters, 119	About this time Capt. Wolaston plants settlement in Massachusetts. Morton one of the Company, 158
Lyford and Oldham called to account, 120	
Lyford, abjectly confessing, is allowed to remain six months on probation, 124	

Events in History of Plymouth	Contemporary Events
1624. Oldham expelled Pinnace recovered at Damarin's Cove sent back to England, 129 Lyford sends more letters of complaint to adventurers	
1625. Oldham returns and is again expelled, 130 Lyford sent to Natasco, 133 The adventurers write expressing dissatisfaction and intention to dissolve the Company, 134-136 A ship and pinnace returning to England taken by Turks almost within sight of Plymouth, 137 Capt. Standish, sent as agent to London,: borrows 150*l.* at 50 per cent. Peace at home, 138 Extension of trade northward Corn sent to Kenebec, 138	1625. *March* 27. *Accession, and June* 22, *First Parliament of Charles I. Wallenstein victorious at Dessau and Tilly at Lutter* — Aug. Plague "very hot" in London, 138
1626. Standish returns; brings news of death of Mr. Robinson and Mr. Cushman Colony having sunk to lowest, begins to rise again, 140 Fishing abandoned for trade in corn, which becomes valuable commodity Goods purchased of moribund colony in Monahigen, 141 And from French ship wrecked at Damarin's Cove, 141 Mr. Allerton sent to England to compound with adventurers, 141	1626. *Feb. Second Parliament of Charles I. Impeachment of Buckingham*
1627. Mr. Allerton returns, having borrowed 200*l.* at 30 per cent., 143 And made bargain with the adventurers for purchase of the property for 1,800*l.* by yearly payments of 200*l.*, 144 All the colonists become shareholders, 145 Division of land by lot, 146 Ship wrecked in Manamoiac.	

Events in History of Plymouth	*Contemporary Events*
Bay. Mr Fells and Mr. Sibsie allowed to settle temporarily, but afterwards dismissed, 148	
1627. Station planted at Manamet (*head of Buzzard's Bay*), 149 Letters and messengers from Dutch at New Amsterdam offering friendship and trade, 150 Proposal of Bradford and two others to form partnership to hire trade of colony for six years	
1628. Allerton concludes partnership with Sherley and others, 154–157 A house erected at Kenibeck, 157 Visit of de Rasiers and others from New Amsterdam, 157 They suggest trade in Whampam, which becomes valuable commodity, 158 Indians beginning to understand use of guns, 158 Morton, in Massachusetts, guilty of gross excesses, becomes source of danger	1628. *Third Parliament of Charles I. Petition of Right* *Mr. John Endicott plants colony at Salem*
Isolated settlers beg colonists of Plymouth to remove him, 161 Morton apprehended and sent to England, 162 Allerton begins private trade, 163	— *Oct.* 10. *Fall of La Rochelle*
1629. A new patent applied for by the partners, 166 Ashley, sent by the London partners, settles at Penobscot, 170 A "bargain of salt"¹ housed near Penobscot leads to the suggestion that a fishing ship should be sent to take it up, 171	1629. Mar. Patent granted to Massachusetts Company
— Mr. Ralfe Smith, coming as a visitor, stays as minister, 172	

¹ This incident was important, as the suggestion that a ship should be sent to take it up occasioned the sending of the *White Angel*, in which Mr. Allerton led the London partners into furthering unwittingly some private schemes of his own, resulting in disagreement, and confusion which was never fully cleared up.

Events in History of Plymouth	Contemporary Events
1629. Aug. Arrival at Salem of some of the Leyden party in the *Talbot*, 165	
1630. May. Arrival at Charlestown of remainder of Leyden party in the *Mayflower*, 165 The first capital punishment, on John Billington, for murder	**1630.** *June. Arrival of 900 emigrants to establish colony of Massachusetts: Mr. John Winthrop governor. Settlement at Charlestown, at Boston, and New-town* — Aug. Visitation of sickness at Charles-town Advice sought from Plymouth, 181
1631. July 14.[1] A fishing ship (*Friend-ship*) arrives at Boston bringing Mr. Hatherley, 176 — July 22.[1] A trading ship (*White Angel*) arrives at Massachusetts Bay bringing Mr. Allerton, 176 Mr. Allerton discharged from the Company Penobscot settlement robbed by the French, who by a ruse take advantage of the servants left in charge, 188 Allerton in the *White Angel* tries to intercept the trade and to make settlement beyond Penobscot, but is foiled by the French, 189 Sir Christopher Gardner, fleeing from consequence of misdeeds at Boston, is captured among the Indians, brought to Ply-mouth, and forwarded to Boston, 198 (a)	
1632. Growth in prosperity and exten-sion of the colony leads to	**1632.** Sir Christopher Gardner appeals to

[1] These events are placed by Bradford in the year 1630. But Mr. Prince, in manuscript annotations, ascribes them to the year 1631, and they are accordingly so placed here. The *White Angel* business resulted in long and troubled correspondence, which fills many pages of Bradford's MS.

Events in History of Plymouth	*Contemporary Events*
separation of Church at Duxbury, 192	Privy Council, which upholds colonists, 190 (a)
1632. And planting of farms at Green's Harbour, 192	
Mr. Pierce comes out in the *Lion*, and returning *viâ* Virginia with 800*l.* of beaver, &c., is wrecked, 193	1632. *Oct.* 16. *Battle of Lützen*
1633. Mr. Edward Winslow governor Roger Williams at Plymouth, 195	1633. Feb. 11. Burning of London Bridge, 194
Settlement on Connecticut River threatened by the Dutch, 196	*Death of Archbishop Abbott*
Visitation of an infectious fever presaged by plague of great flies, 197	*Wm. Laud archbishop*
3,366 lb. of beaver and 346 other skins sent home, 197	
1634. Mr. Thomas Prence governor	
Hocking, from Pascataway, tries to intercept the trade at Kenibeck, 199	
In the conflict which ensued Hocking kills an Indian and is killed by another	
Disputes arise, 200	
The ministers of neighbouring colonies invited by Winthrop to meet at Boston and arbitrate : the men of Plymouth exonerated, 202	— April 28. A decree of the Privy Council constitutes the Archbishop and others a commission for the government of the colonies, with full powers to make laws for organisation of Church and State, 201 (a)
Captain Stone tries to carry off a Plymouth ship from Connecticut : fails ; is subsequently killed by Indians, 203 (a)	
Visitation of smallpox and sickness, fatal to Indians, but English escape	
1635. Bradford governor	
Winslow comes to England to notify the end of the partnership, 205	
Appeals to Privy Council against encroachment of French and Dutch, 205	Design of Archbishop to establish episcopal government of Church in colonies, 206
French under Mons. de Aulnoye seize settlement at Penobscot, 207	

"MAYFLOWER" ESSAYS

145

Events in History of Plymouth	Contemporary Events
1635. A ship hired to dispossess them, but without success, 208	
Boston invited to co operate to drive them out, but declines, 209	
— Aug. 14 or 15. A mighty storm of wind and rain, 210	
Disagreement with Dorchester about Connecticut: compromise with Dorchester for peace' sake, 211	1635. Beginnings of (Baptist) colony at Providence
1636. Mr. Edward Winslow governor	1636. Distress owing to the Plague in London, 215
Misfortunes to Massachusetts trade in Connecticut suggest a "judgment" on their selfishness	1626. Hampden refuses "ship money"
Pequents try to make friendship with colonists of Massachusetts, but are refused, 219	Attempt to enforce Prayer Book in Scotland
Begin aggressions on English, 219	Hartford, Windsor, and Weatherfield in Connecticut colonised from Massachusetts
1637. Bradford governor	
Pequents make open war on Connecticut	
Boston invites help from Plymouth	
Narrigansets refuse to join their old enemies the Pequents, who are annihilated: some fly to Mohawks, some to Monhiggs (Mohicans), 223-225	
1638. Mr. Thomas Prence governor	1638. Settlement at Aquednek, Rhode Island
Three men executed for murder of an Indian, 228	
Prosperity and high prices at Plymouth, 229	Scotch covenant renewed
— June 1 or 2. Earthquake, 230	First settlements at Newhaven
First prison, 230	
1639. Bradford governor	
1640. Dispute and commission to settle boundaries of Sityate and Hingham, 231	1640. Nov. 3. Opening of "Long Parliament"
Bradford resigns his patent	
Sudden collapse in prices	
1641. Final wind-up of partnership.	

L

Events in History of Plymouth	*Contemporary Events*
Colony pays 1,200*l.* in full quittance to London partners	1641. *May* 12. *Execution of Strafford*
1641. Mr. Chancy, a minister, raises question of baptism by immersion, 240	
Churches of Boston, Connecticut, and New Haven decide against it, 241	
Troubles and depression in colony: thoughts of removal, 241	
1642. Boston consults Plymouth about defiant attitude of "Anabaptists and Familists" at Aquednek, 242	1642. *Beginning of Civil War in England*
And other grievous immoralities. Execution of an offender, 249	— *Nov.* 12. *Battle of Edgehill*
1643. April 16. Death of Brewster, 253	1643-48. *Westminster Assembly*
Confederacy for mutual defence (against Narrigansets) between Massachusetts, Plymouth, Connecticut, and New Haven	1643. *May* 14. *Accession of Louis XIV.*
United Colonies of New England, 256	— *June* 24. *Death of Hampden at Chalgrove Field*
Uncass of Monhiggs, with English help, defeats Myantinomo of Narrigansets and executes him, 260	
1644. Mr. Edward Winslow governor	1644. *July* 2. *Battle of Marston Moor*
Renewed projects of removal to Nawset, 261	
Murder of English people near Connecticut, 262	*Rise of Independents in Parliament*
Temporary agreement with Indians to keep quiet, 263	
1645. July 28. Meeting of commissioners of united colonies at Boston, 264	1645. *Jan.* 10. *Execution of Archbishop Laud*
War threatening with Narrigansets. Seaconk garrisoned, 265	— J u n e. Battle of Naseby
Before hostilities break out commissioners sent	
Peace concluded between united colonies and Indians, 268	
1646. Bradford governor	
Arrival of three ships under Capt. Crumwell, 269	
Winslow returns to England	
1647-1648.	

Spottiswoode & Co. Printers, New-street Square, London.

A Reproduction in fac-simile, by Photography, of the original Manuscript of

THE HISTORY

OF THE

PLIMOTH PLANTATION

WRITTEN BY

WILLIAM BRADFORD,

One of the Founders of, and Second Governor of that Colony.

WITH AN INTRODUCTION BY

JOHN A. DOYLE,

Fellow of All Souls' College, Oxford.

———

LONDON: WARD & DOWNEY, LIMITED.
BOSTON: HOUGHTON MIFFLIN & CO.
1896.

———

THE Manuscript contains an account of the Settlement in Holland, first at Amsterdam, and afterwards at Leyden, of the Community of Puritan Separatists commonly known as Brownists; of their departure from Holland and embarkation at Southampton in 1620 in the ship 'May-flower'; of the voyage of the 'Pilgrim Fathers' in the

'Mayflower' to America ; of the foundation by them there of 'Plimoth Plantation,' and of the history and government of the Plantation until 1646.

It contains also : 'The names of those which came over first, in the year 1620, and were (by the blessing of God) the first beginners, and (in a sort) the foundation of all the plantations and Colonies in New England (and their families).'

The Manuscript belongs to the Library at Fulham Palace. It has been conjectured that it was brought to England at the time of the American War ; but there is no reference to its existence in America later than 1767. Up to 1854 American students of the history of their country failed to trace it, and Dr. Young in his 'Chronicles of the Pilgrim Fathers' (published in 1841) refers to it as 'hopelessly lost.' Attention was, however, in 1854, directed to its resting-place by passages and citations in 'A History of the Protestant Episcopal Church of America,' by Samuel Wilberforce, Bishop of Oxford. Leave was obtained to transcribe the MS., and it was published by the Massachusetts Historical Society in their 'Collections' in 1856.

The MS. consists of 280 folio pages, in William Bradford's own handwriting, and is an example of clear and beautiful penmanship. Messrs. Ward & Downey believe that the reproduction in fac-simile of a work of so peculiar an interest and value will be highly esteemed by scholars and collectors.

The edition is limited to 350 copies, printed on fine hand-made paper, and each copy is numbered.

STUDIES

OF

CONTEMPORARY SUPERSTITIONS.

By W. H. MALLOCK.

1 vol. crown 8vo. buckram.   Price 6s.

CONTENTS :—The Scientific Bases of Optimism—'Cowardly Agnos-
ticism ' — Amateur Christianity—Marriage and Free Thought—
A Catholic Theologian on Natural Religion—Science and the
Revolution—Fabian Economics—The So-called Evolution of
Socialism.

PRESS OPINIONS.

' A brilliant attempt to combat the Agnosticism of the day with its own weapons.
TIMES.

' It deals, with all the force and cleverness which mark Mr. Mallock's works,
with some aspects of the great questions, religious and social, which occupy so much
space in contemporary thought.'—SPECTATOR.

' A remarkable work from a close reasoner and valiant champion.'
ST. JAMES'S GAZETTE.

' One of the ablest and one of the most readable of the productions of the
believing sceptics and Christian agnostics.'—GLASGOW HERALD.

' Undoubtedly of great contemporary interest.'—ABERDEEN FREE PRESS.

' A fierce indictment, but we must confess that Mr. Mallock makes out a very
strong case.   He rolls his enemies in the dust with an amazing zest and a very stout
pair of arms. . . . It is when he comes to deal with the Superstitions of Socialism
that Mr. Mallock is at his best.'—SATURDAY REVIEW.

' We have nothing but praise for this volume.'—CHURCH TIMES.

' The article on " Amateur Christianity " is a particularly just and adroit piece
of reasoning.'—THE GUARDIAN.

WARD & DOWNEY, Ltd., 12 York Buildings, Adelphi, W.C

SOME
CELEBRATED IRISH BEAUTIES
OF THE
LAST CENTURY.

By FRANCES GERARD.

Sketches of the Lives of Mary Molesworth (Countess of Belvedere), Eleanor Ambrose ('The Dangerous Papist'), the Gunnings (Maria, Countess of Coventry; Elizabeth, Duchess of Hamilton and of Argyll; Kitty Gunning, and Gunilda Gunning), Peg Woffington, Dorothea Monroe, the Three Montgomerys (Annie, Marchioness of Townshend; Elizabeth, Lady Mountjoy; and Barbara, Mrs. Beresford), Elizabeth La Touche (Countess of Lanesborough), Anne Luttrell (Duchess of Cumberland), the Coghlans of Ardo (Anne, Countess of Barrymore; Eliza, Duchesse de Castries, &c.), Miss Farren (Countess of Derby), &c.

With numerous Portraits and Illustrations. One vol. demy 8vo.

Price 21s.

PRESS OPINIONS.

'When true stories of a past time are told by one who can set them forth in all the grace of a good literary style they are infused with a finer charm than any romance. These stories possess that charm in a remarkable degree.'—ACADEMY.

'I well remember the interest and pleasure with which I read your biography of the excellent Angelica Kauffmann, and I am receiving a somewhat similar enjoyment in the perusal of your "Irish Beauties."'—From a letter to the Author written by the Right Hon. W. E. GLADSTONE.

'Miss Gerard has had an ample store on which to draw; and as she has not been reticent concerning both the virtues and the failings of her heroines, her volume is interesting and piquant reading.'—ST. JAMES'S GAZETTE.

'Very attractive and readable. It is full of bright, gay gossip, and often gives us a vivid picture of a bygone England.'—PALL MALL GAZETTE.

'A gallery of portraits and a collection of memoirs in one handsome volume.'
THE WORLD.
'Full of entertaining and valuable information.'—NATIONAL OBSERVER.

WARD & DOWNEY, Ltd., 12 York Buildings, Adelphi, W.C.

IN A WALLED GARDEN.

By MADAME BESSIE RAYNER BELLOC.

Personal Recollections of George Eliot, Mary Howitt, Basil Montagu, Adelaide Procter, Mrs. Jameson, Lady Georgiana Fullerton, Comte Adolphe de Circourt, Cardinal Manning, Mrs. Booth, &c.

1 vol. crown 8vo. price 6s. Third Edition.

PRESS OPINIONS.

'A fascinating book. One of the sunniest, freshest, and, in the highest sense, most entertaining of volumes.'—LITERARY WORLD.

'Bright and intelligent from cover to cover.'—DAILY CHRONICLE.

'Full of anecdote and of personal touches which seem to make the personality of each subject start to new life.'—THE WORLD.

'Very pleasantly written and informing essays about people of whom one is glad to hear. Madame Belloc's brief and exact history, with its appreciative criticisms, takes us over three generations.'—THE TIMES.

'Of high merit and interest. A volume that is well worth reading.'
ABERDEEN FREE PRESS.

'A garden that we like. An attractive and interesting book.'
PALL MALL GAZETTE.

'One of the most interesting books of the season.'—THE NEW AGE.

'The whole volume . . . bears witness to the refinement and knowledge of its author.'—THE SPEAKER.

'I have closed this dainty and attractive volume with feelings of gratitude for the gentle and kindly lady who has permitted me to wander through her walled garden. . . . Many others will doubtless take advantage of the same privilege.'
THE ACADEMY.

'Madame Belloc's judgments upon her friends are less acute, or penetrative, or flashing than discriminating, sympathetic, and appreciative; her aim being rather to present the agreeable and attractive qualities they exhibited in family and social life than to make a dissertation or analysis of their qualities. The most fresh and interesting pages are those in which the writer gives her impressions of Adelaide Procter.'—ST. JAMES'S GAZETTE.

WARD & DOWNEY, Ltd., 12 York Buildings, Adelphi, W.C.

ANNOUNCEMENTS.

Messrs. WARD & DOWNEY, Ltd., have in the press an important work on the Pilgrim Fathers and the Foundation and History of the New England Colonies, by Professor E. ARBER. The book will be entitled—

THE STORY OF
THE PILGRIM FATHERS.

1607–1630 A.D.

AS TOLD BY

THEMSELVES, THEIR FRIENDS, AND THEIR ENEMIES.

By EDWARD ARBER, F.S.A.

Hon. Member of the Virginia and Wisconsin Historical Societies ; late English Examiner at the London University, and also at the Victoria University, Manchester ; Emeritus Professor of English Language and Literature, Mason College, Birmingham.

It will be published in November in One Volume.

Messrs. WARD & DOWNEY, Ltd., have in the press Miss FRANCES GERARD'S New Book, entitled

SOME
CELEBRATED IRISH BEAUTIES

OF THE

PRESENT CENTURY.

This will be a companion volume to the same Author's **'SOME CELEBRATED IRISH BEAUTIES OF THE LAST CENTURY,'** and will contain Sketches of the Lives of Mrs. Dorothea Jordan—Lady Anne and Lady Gertrude Fitzpatrick—Sarah Curran—Anne Birmingham (Countess of Charlemont), and her Sister (Countess of Leitrim)— Mrs. Chenevix Trench—Sidney Owenson (Lady Morgan)—Olivia Owenson (Lady Clarke)—Mrs. Norton—Miss O'Neill—Lola Montez— Marguerite Power (Countess of Blessington).

The volume will contain several Portraits and other Illustrations, and will be issued in demy 8vo. at One Guinea.

WARD & DOWNEY, Ltd., 12 York Buildings, Adelphi, W.C.

www.ingramcontent.com/pod-product-compliance
Lightning Source LLC
Chambersburg PA
CBHW020554270326
41927CB00006B/836